THIS IS
A MINEFIELD

By Aaron Chan

Signal 8 Press
Hong Kong

Praise for *This City Is a Minefield*:

"Soulful and intimate, Aaron Chan's debut slips us between lives. By turns comic and wrenching, *The City Is a Minefield* is the remembrance of an ongoing search; in unanticipated ways, in revelatory moments, he finds ways to both survive in, and reimagine, our world."

— Madeleine Thien, author of *Do Not Say We Have Nothing;* winner of the Giller Prize and the Governor General's Award (Canada)

"Aaron Chan's voice is both tender and commanding as he leads you through *This City Is A Minefield*. Sit with him in front of his parents' '70s Zenith console TV to watch Chinese soap operas or follow him through the steam-filled maze of a gay bathhouse. Wherever he takes you, he does with unflinching openness. A captivating debut—I'll follow Chan anywhere."

— Amber Dawn, author of *How Poetry Saved My Life: A Hustler's Memoir*

"A searing collection of contemplative and autobiographical musings that confront the challenges of a young gay man's life with astonishing courage and candour. You won't be able to put it down."

— Andreas Schroeder, author of the autobiographical novel *Renovating Heaven*

"*This City Is a Minefield* is a smart and beautiful collection of autobiographical essays that movingly captures and explores the gay Asian experience in the West, as Aaron negotiates and navigates the tumultuous terrain of representation and intersection of sexual identity and race—the heartbreaks, the joys, and above all, the resilience. My only wish after reading it is that the book had been published much earlier so that my younger self could have devoured and learned from it!"

— Edward Gunawan, writer-filmmaker

"*This City Is a Minefield* is a well-considered and insightful rumination on Vancouver, one that both challenges and confirms its reality as a city that is multicultural in its makeup, but haunted by an enduring legacy of white hegemony—publicly, privately, and sexually. Aaron Chan's voice is one that we urgently need, and thankfully have, in the form of this critical new memoir."

— Wayde Compton, author of *The Outer Harbour*

"In *This City is a Minefield,* Aaron Chan has drawn an honest, moving portrait of what it means to live and grow up as a 'third-culture' kid in Vancouver's Cantonese and gay communities—and what it means to feel never Canadian enough, never Chinese enough, and never beautiful enough to love and be loved. In crisp, spare prose, Chan strikes familiar notes in the Asian diasporic narrative while adding his own distinctive counterpoint meditations on the meaning of purpose, desire, and beauty. This is a lasting contribution to the growing canon of Asian queer literature, and a must-read for all of us who have struggled to know the meaning of home."

— Kai Cheng Thom, author of *I Hope We Choose Love: A Trans Girl's Notes From the End of the World*

This City Is a Minefield

By Aaron Chan
Published by Signal 8 Press
An imprint of Signal 10 Media, Inc.
Copyright 2019 Aaron Chan
ISBN: 978-988-77949-1-2

Signal 8 Press
Website: www.signal8press.com
Hong Kong

Lyrics from the following songs have been reprinted. All reasonable efforts have been made to contact the copyright holders.

© 1971 "A Case of You" Joni Mitchell Publishing Corp., ASCAP. Written by Joni Mitchell.
© 2010 "Cold War" Ink is an Instrument Publishing, Jane Lle Publishing, Tang Nivri Publishing, ASCAP, NS. Written by Nathaniel Irvin, Charles Delbert Joseph, Janelle Monáe Robinson.
© 2010 "On the Ocean" Campfire Sky Music, Low Crawl Music, ASCAP. Written by Adam Gardner, Ryan Miller, Joseph Pisapia, and Brian Rosenworcel.

Cover design: Manuela di Gioia
Art direction: Cristian Checcanin
Author photo: Erin Flegg

To Curtis (blurtis)

This City Is a Minefield – Aaron Chan

TABLE OF CONTENTS

THIS CITY

MAYBE it's just the way everyone grows up, but I never thought of my city as a particularly different or special place. I didn't feel lucky or privileged or complacent. Vancouver was just what it was.

Full disclosure: I was born in Burnaby, a suburb just outside of Vancouver, but I tell everyone I'm from Vancouver because it's where my family moved shortly after I was born and where I grew up. I think part of my feeling like Vancouver was the way it was for me was that I was a kid growing up on the West Side—in the snobby, middle-upper-class district of Kerrisdale, to be specific—and the little bubble I inhabited. My limited knowledge of the world consisted of buildings and the rooms and spaces within them. My elementary school, Maple Grove Elementary, was a mere half block away from my family's three-story house. I also walked to the local community centre often, where I learned to swim; I scoured bookstacks for tiny, hidden pictures in the library downstairs for prizes during their Summer Reading Club program; and I began my very first piano lessons with a young woman named Monique. Particularly exciting and always surprising because we never paid attention to them until they were happening were Kerrisdale Days: all along the cobblestoned sidewalk of 41st Avenue, tents and tables were set out from storefronts offering free popcorn and cotton candy, balloons with company logos printed on them, and for the adults, various sales. Sidewalks were abuzz with families, children, and strollers; there was a lot of squeezing, careful maneuvering, and side-stepping involved. Ponies shouldered giggling children on the trails adjacent to the railroad tracks along East Boulevard (though I never got to ride on a pony because my parents feared animals and contact was forbidden, much to my dismay). To me, my city was pretty neat (I mean, ponies and candy! Come on!).

On Saturday mornings, my parents drove me and my two older sisters to Chinese school, which was held at a high school. Classes were taught in Cantonese by teachers who spoke little to no English, which made for fantastic learning and communication when I often could only phrase questions in English. To signal recess, a student walked up and down the halls clanging a metal bell—I assumed that was what Chinese schools in Hong Kong and China were like because the high school did have a PA system. For the most part, I loathed going to Chinese School. I found it tedious and boring, the stories we read so bland and bluntly moralistic, not to mention rewriting passages from memory was utterly useless in learning the language. And because the classes gave writing and reading formal Chinese priority over conversational speaking, it was probably the reason why my oral skills barely developed. Mostly, I just sat at my desk and tried my best to look inconspicuous and somewhat attentive so I wouldn't be called on to answer questions. In all honesty, I probably picked up most of my Cantonese at home, talking with and listening to my Chinese parents (i.e. all the insults that were yelled at me and my siblings). When I think about my time studying Chinese, it triggers conflicting emotions: nostalgia mixed with disgust.

Three long hours later, my parents awaited us around the corner in my dad's dull-grey '88 Honda—bought the same year my twin sister Maggie and I were born. Sometimes, we had noodles and congee for lunch at a Chinese restaurant, though I have fond memories of my mother making instant noodles for us at home while we set the table. The kitchen windows fogged up from the combination of rain outside and steamy food inside (it was probably days like these that eventually conditioned me to enjoy staying home warm and cozy when it rained, which was often).

In addition to schools and sidewalks, there were a few other landmarks in my world: my grandparents' house in East Van off Broadway, where Grandpa always offered me and my twin sister a can of seasoned peanuts, and my paternal grandparents' house in Renfrew where I would gleefully punch in imaginary transactions on an old cash register in the basement; grocery shopping and getting my hair cut in noisy, bustling Chinatown; and nestled in Strathcona, Great-Grandma and her retirement home, where she sometimes literally threw money at me to keep when we visited.

If you had asked me when I was young to draw you a map of Vancouver, it would have looked like a sparse collection of tiny circles on a blank page, dotted stars amidst the otherwise black of the unknown universe. I am kind of embarrassed to admit it, but it took me a while to acquaint myself with my own town.

My three-story house and former farm was the common

denominator for most of my memories: Maggie and I fighting one minute, and the next, me yelling down the hall, asking if she wanted to play again; combing through the plastic-covered, dry-cleaned dresses and jackets hanging in our cramped little attic/storage room before concealing myself behind them during a game of hide and seek; my other, older sister Florence and I sneaking pretzels and chips in her locked basement bedroom and chatting and laughing about school; digging out old boxes of Christmas decorations and holiday VHS movies in the laundry room (that I now wonder why we even possessed at all); practicing scales and triad chords on the Yamaha upright piano; sprinting up the mustard-yellow, woolly carpeted stairs to the safety of my parents' locked room when Florence threatened to strike me with the long bamboo handle of the rainbow-feathered duster, our family's disciplinary weapon; helping my dad sweep up fresh grass trimmings and gazing up in awe at the towering rows of beanstalks in our backyard. I frequently had dreams about the house, in which I usually ran away from someone or something (I still do). I thought our house would be around forever.

We kids always complained about the house—the sub-zero basement year-round was our main gripe—but when I was twelve, my parents returned one night from the realtor's office to announce they had sold the house, it stunned me. Despite it having been on the market for a while, I never imagined they would really be able to sell our home. I thought it was a plot to appease us whining kids for a while before calling the whole thing off. A joke.

But they had done it, and it wasn't funny. I couldn't conceive of what not living in that house would mean. Where would we live? How would we live? I was afraid of expanding my bubble into the other parts of a city I wasn't familiar with, not to mention parting with my childhood home and potentially, my neighbourhood.

Shortly following the sale of my childhood home, my parents announced that they were separating. After years of estrangement despite living under the same roof, no one was surprised by this. I think I wasn't quite sure how to process this news. I felt like there was an expectation to be devastated and melodramatic the way I had seen kids react on television when their parents announced their decision. I'm sure I did feel some sort of remorse that my family was now officially broken, but there was a stoic acceptance of the fact. Plus, my sisters both seemed indifferent as well.

While my father moved in with his parents in Renfrew, my sisters and I stayed with Mom, whom we were much closer with. After briefly renting a haunted basement suite further south in Kerrisdale (seriously, I'm pretty sure it was haunted; just ask my mom about the voice singing opera in the middle of the night), we occasionally visited a giant mound of dirt on the other side of town, in East Van, and over some months watched as it progressively transformed itself into a real house. I was vaguely aware of the neighbourhood, as my maternal grandparents had moved nearby a few years back. Upon my first ventures, the neighborhood appeared to be blocks of Chinese bakeries, Chinese markets, and Chinese herbs and dried goods shops. And lots of old Chinese people. It definitely wasn't as glamorous (and white) as Kerrisdale, but there was something about it that felt familiar, safe. I loved the quirky, obliviously unironic sense of humour it had: a cafe that was also a pharmacy; a small grocery store that sold cigarettes and tea next to aquarium supplies; a handwritten sign at a walk-in clinic that read, "Free 'flu' shots." The neighbourhood felt down to earth, modest, and unpretentious. Needless to say, I adjusted quickly after we moved in. Kerrisdale became a faint but fond memory not too long after.

Our house also had the advantage of being somewhat central and easily accessible to the rest of the city. Taking the #20 bus, I wound my way to Commercial Drive—dubbed The Drive by Vancouverites—and was intrigued by young rebels with neon hair and leather jackets with faithful street dogs at their sides. During my high school years, I wandered downtown on weekends for hours where I eagerly flipped through sheet music at Tom Lee Music or scouted out the latest deals at the HMV megastore. The more I explored the city, the more amazed I was; I loved what it had to offer: my high school friends; many different parks; tasty cuisine from all over the world; places where I could get music; petrichor, the unmistakable soft scent of rain as it began to fall. Vancouver was a place where you could find everything you could find elsewhere and yet nowhere else, like a special trading card with unique abilities. I was proud to say that I was from here.

As everyone started to prepare their university applications in the months leading up to high school graduation, I found myself suddenly wondering what I was going to do with my life. I really didn't feel like continuing several years' worth of education since high school had worn me out. The image of sitting inside more classrooms for at least another four years, listening to professors drone on and on about subjects I had no interest in—my idea of university life—nauseated me. My friends were going on to higher education but most didn't know what they wanted to do.

My Chinese parents, of course, demanded that I go to school, preferably at the University of British Columbia, which Florence had also attended. I did not think UBC was that great. Florence had graduated but was still searching for a job, and one not even related to what she had studied. I tried citing her as an example of why I shouldn't go to university, but my mother wasn't having it. As the nagging continued day after day, week after week, it was beginning to feel like my entire existence—and by extension, living in Vancouver—was to go school and appease my parents, things I did not want. I felt like Vancouver had lured me in like a car salesman, spouting a comfortable ride, only to point out the fine print and the dozens of strings attached.

Aware of my stubbornness, my mom became a fraction more flexible. "I don't care where you study. Just go study somewhere and learn something," she pleaded.

If my parents were going to force me to go school, I was going to study something *I* wanted to study. Something like... music. A couple of music courses at Vancouver Community College, for a start. Take that, conservative Chinese parents! As everyone expected, they were dismayed at my decision, but I didn't care. Vancouver and I kissed and made up.

After that, my relationship status with the city evolved into something deeper.

I had been playing the piano since I was five and playing and singing pop songs (mostly at home) since I was fifteen. To say the least, contemporary songs were leagues more entertaining than music written 150 years ago. At seventeen, I wrote my first song, titled "Empty" (I'm sure you can guess what it was about). Songwriting seemed like a fun and natural mix of music and writing, both of which I had enjoyed since I was a kid. Despite Maggie ordering, "No singing!" whenever I practiced at home, I felt drive and passion alight in me in my music. Then I had what I thought was the most brilliant idea.

I was going to be a singer-songwriter.

When my father found out I wanted to be a musician, he stated, rather flatly, "I don't think it will work out for you." Once, he related a story to me. "You have a kid who says, 'Daddy, I'm hungry.' And you tell him, 'I'm sorry, son. I don't have any money to buy food.' That is what is going to happen to you." Similarly, my mom, asked, "Who is going to listen to your music? You are no one, just playing around. Piano is only supposed to be a hobby." Their discouragement only motivated me further.

From my first performance at seventeen and for the following few years, I performed at local venues, mostly cafes, to handfuls of people: Myles of Beans in Burnaby, Trees Organic Coffee downtown, the Rhizome Cafe. Other times, I was asked by friends and colleagues to perform at events. There were—and still are—so many musicians in the city that it truly felt like a community. When I found an online listing of open mic venues around Metro Vancouver, I was as giddy as a *Twilight* fangirl. I joined a music organization dedicated to assisting musicians of all levels. The hosts of the open mic night at Myles of Beans offered me gift certificates for studio time at a professional music studio to record my songs. Whenever I lugged around my cumbersome, massive keyboard to venues, I felt important, like my music and I belonged to the local music scene. One time, I performed with Wanting Qu at Trees before she racked up millions of views on YouTube. Yes, I was part of the artists struggling to make a living doing my art. How many of my former high school classmates could say the same? (Well, someone managed to win a Juno Award a few years later, so one. At least that I know of.)

During every performance, my mouth always became parched, which made it difficult to sing, but performing was nevertheless a thrill. My friends, my sister, and even my mom on a few occasions, came to watch me perform (my dad, however, has never come to my shows). With the help of a producer, I recorded a four-song demo one day and began handing them out, then selling them. If there was a city to become famous as a musician, I felt like Vancouver was where it was at. Michael Bublé, Nelly Furtado, Nickelback—okay, I knew I wasn't going to be as big and famous as any of them, but they all started from the ground up too. It might take a while, but it could happen.

It had been a few months since my brief semester at community college, which didn't turn out to be as fun and interesting as I had hoped. Once again, my parents unsubtly nudged me—nay, kicked me in the butt—to pursue higher education.

Common phrases from Mom: "You have had fun with

your music. Now it is time to stop playing around and get serious"; "You think you know everything, but you know nothing"; "You are falling behind all your friends in university. They are graduating soon!"; and "Think about UBC. Mom is not trying to harm you."

I understood my mom's reasoning/nagging, but I was still not feeling it. I did not want to trap myself in a program and make myself miserable for years. Studying music might not truly be my calling, but I did like movies and writing. And for some time, I wanted to adapt my favourite teen novel for the big screen but never knew how or where to start.

Then came my second idea.

To my parents' horror yet again, I enrolled in Vancouver Film School's Screenwriting Program. Although they begrudgingly paid the pricey tuition with money they had saved in an education savings account for years, they did not hesitate to let me know what they thought.

"What are you going to do when you graduate? What kind of job can you get? What *can* you do? I think you are wasting your life," my dad said with a sigh and a shake of the head that I had now identified as his trademark. "But don't say I didn't warn you." It was easy to not take my father's words seriously. He didn't even truly know me, so I didn't expect him to understand my passions.

In film school, I eagerly learned to write scripts and screenplays, developed a TV pilot, and graduated with a short film I wrote—my "port-short" (portfolio short). Once more, that instinct of "This is the right path for me" arose, which I took as a meaningful sign. I participated in a documentary project called Playing It Safe with a local organization and made a series of shorts. Film suddenly became endlessly inspiring and full of potential. Plus, I continued writing my own music and incorporated it in my work too. I felt as if film was the perfect marriage of all my artistic abilities.

Vancouver is famous for all the film productions year-round, most notably the American ones that turn the city into Los Angeles or New York or anywhere else except Vancouver. As with music, there is a small but significant indie film scene in the city; filmmakers, actors, and eager crew are out there—if you live in Vancouver, chances are, you already know someone involved in film in some capacity. After graduating from film school and connecting with the filmmakers from the documentary project, it was easy to feel like Vancouver would equally support me if I went into making movies.

So I did. My port-short, *On the Bus,* eventually screened at various international film festivals, and though I had no formal training, I forced myself to become a director in order to get my name out there (let's face it: no one cares about the *writer* of short films—or any films, really). With the help of friends who were willing to volunteer long hours on film sets, I made— wrote, directed, edited, produced, casted, composed music for, etc.—several gay-themed short films. All of them were accepted by and premiered at the Vancouver Queer Film Festival. The cherry on top was getting paid a screening fee from the festival. It wasn't a fortune by any means, but it made me feel like I could legitimately make money from the art I created. It was an encouraging start.

Other awesome things: I had the amazing opportunity to

introduce my films in front of packed houses at the Vancouver
Queer Film Festival; one year, I sat on a panel discussing the
difficulties of being an artist of colour; I was invited to do interviews by local organizations; like-minded artists constantly
inspired me. Audiences seemed to enjoy my films (although I
will say that they unexpectedly laughed at parts in a dramatic
film I made). I began getting the feeling that my name was
slowly, but surely, becoming one that people in the film scene,
or at least in the queer community, recognized. It was all such
an adventure. Best of all, being a filmmaker felt like more solid footing than being a musician. It paid ever so slightly more
than the donations I received for my music demos.

Although my parents supported my schooling financially,
they were always frowning upon my musical or film endeav-
ours. My dad, in particular, continued to tell me he didn't think
I would make it and repeatedly suggested, "People are getting
old and will need care. You can make money as a physiotherapist. Think about it." (I have no interest in physiotherapy.)

"This road that you are taking is very hard. If it was easy,
everyone would do it. Why don't you be a doctor or a dentist
or a lawyer?" my mom has said. Unless I did what they wanted, I knew my parents were never going to approve of my life.
Unlike them, the city seemed to understand me.

I owed Vancouver for being the supportive parent I never
had.

***

And the people. Of course the people.

Friendly. Polite. A mosaic of the world.

Maybe the fact that everyone is so different is the reason why I never felt out of place in my city. I have read memoirs and personal stories of people of colour being the only minority in their towns, how they experienced racism and bullying and because of that, were ashamed of their culture and heritage. But it was never the case for me. Growing up, life was pretty normal. I don't recall ever being harassed for being Chinese. In elementary school, my classmates and I played soccer during lunch break: we were white, yellow, brown—it didn't matter. We all got along. Race was a complete non-issue when we were kids. My class photos—with all sorts of different faces smiling back—was proof enough of that. The city was abundant in immigrant families, and with their kids kicking soccer balls around with other kids, I can see why they would think Vancouver was a pleasant place to live.

On top of that, everyone seemed to be pretty easy-going and friendly. We actually knew and spent time with our neighbours in Kerrisdale. Strangers were kind and friendly (although for the longest time I had a borderline phobia of talking to adults); I recall a fun news story with a reporter asking the public what the best thing about Vancouver was and almost everyone answered, "The people." I agreed. I was proud that Vancouverites had such a positive reputation—and that even if it was only a fragment, I contributed to it.

"You are really lucky to live here," my mom told me on more than one occasion, usually as the evening news showed footage of nations senselessly bombing each other to hell or people protesting against their oppressive governments. "You have a house, education, clothes, health care. Good weather. And no natural disasters."

"Except for the earthquake that will kill us all one day," I liked to remind her.

It's not that I never thought that the rest of the world was different from Vancouver, but that it simply had never crossed my mind. *I suppose I am lucky*, I thought to myself.

I think I finally had an opinion about the city I grew up in the day I watched the sun set on a spring night from my bedroom. On a whim, I parted the vertical blinds filtering out the twilight from the convex curve of my bay window. The sky was washed out in saturated yellow and orange hues. Clouds glowed lavender and rose, as if lit from behind by a flame. With the North Shore snow-capped mountains peering over distant shimmering city lights, the view looked as if the sky was a canvas and someone had streaked oil pastels across town, just for the heck of it. The panoramic sight stole my breath—few things do. For a long time, I truly believed this was the most beautiful place on Earth.

And also nostalgic. Artistic. Friendly. Welcoming. Supportive.

So when people used to ask me where I wanted to settle down in the world, my answer was always immediate.

Here. This city.

Vancouver.

Between Channels

THE first gay person I see dies in front of my eyes.

It's 8pm again. I squeal and laugh as the cheesy saxophone theme to *A Kindred Spirit* spills out from our old '70s Zenith console TV in the living room. Clad in my fuzzy pig slippers, my nine-year-old feet sprint for the center spot on the couch before either of my sisters can claim it. The rest of my family is all smiles as they settle down around me, the TV tuned to Fairchild, the Chinese television network in Vancouver.

But this episode tonight is different from the regular family drama that I have been watching for the past few months. When Jackie and Gary appear onscreen for the first time, while my family gasps and sighs appropriately along with the show, I am quiet. I have never seen gay people before, let alone a gay couple. They are like alien creatures I am inexplicably fascinated by; I find myself staring at the screen as if this dramedy show has now become a documentary on the life of a gay person. I hold my breath as Jackie breaks up with Gary and suddenly decides he is no longer gay, proving so by dating a woman named Rebecca. After the show ends for the night, as my family buzzes about Jackie and Gary, I make a few half-hearted remarks instead of joining in as usual.

This happens night after night during the week: I no longer shriek in excitement before the next episode. Instead, I observe intently as Gary tries and fails to talk to Jackie, who wants nothing to do with him anymore. When the program ends for the day, I mumble a few comments, but never say the word "gay." It will be nearly another decade before I can physically say it.

Before the final episode of their story, my family is excited. "Gay Gary, Gay Gary!" my sister Maggie merrily shouts as she races past me and takes the center spot on the dark green leather couch. My family laughs at my sister's joke. I do not.

I drag my feet over. I am apprehensive about Gary's fate since things have not been going well for him. Onscreen, Gary tells Jackie to go to what was once their apartment for their final meeting. The camera pans over the many things in the apartment and ultimately lands on a photo of the couple with their arms around each other, smiling. Then it cuts to Jackie arriving and their inevitable quarrel: Jackie has changed, but Gary isn't going to let him go that easily. As their argument escalates, Gary takes out a big kitchen knife that reminds me of the one we keep in our kitchen drawer.

I watch as Gary stabs his ex-love in the stomach, a violent action which renders him momentarily horrified and distracted. My eyes widen as Jackie, using his last bit of strength, shoves Gary out of the apartment window, where he falls to his death several stories below. Jackie survives the knife attack and goes on to marry Rebecca. The two of them presumably live happily ever after as the show continues (featuring other characters and plots).

I gape at the screen as the credits roll and the theme song plays again. While everyone muses about Gary's death and how Jackie was right to kill his aggressor, I shuffle to the bathroom in a daze, brush my teeth, and get ready for bed without saying a word. In the dark of my room, as I climb into bed, I silently vow, *Well, I'm never telling my family that I'm gay now.*

In the years after *A Kindred Spirit*, I watch less and less Chinese television until eventually stopping altogether. I still love watching series like the adaptation of *Journey to the West*, but as enjoyable and entertaining as they are, they leave me feeling unsatisfied. I can feel and hear a small part of myself softly pawing against the closet door like a cat.

At Chinese school on Saturday mornings, all the stories we read in class involve boys and girls, Chinese families doing everyday things. During dinnertime, reporters recap the news in Cantonese—news that never mentions anything gay or queer. When we have large family potlucks at my relatives' places or at my grandparents' musty little house in East Van, I can't help but notice patterns: aunt and uncle, uncle and aunt, aunt and uncle, grandma and grandpa, female cousins talking about boys and male cousins being teased about not finding girls.

As though I am watching *A Kindred Spirit*, I observe these characters, wondering where my place is in all of this.

I do not come up with an answer.

The yellow-green of the one and two zeros of my alarm clock blind me in the darkness. My hand hovers on the snooze button despite the fact that I am fully awake, but I wait until the last second counts down and the alarm goes off anyway before subduing the noise. After another minute of talking myself through the plan, I extract myself from my bed. In the silent hallway, I tread gently on the wooden floorboards that I have figured out don't creak, tiptoe past the open bathroom and onto the stone-cold tiles of the kitchen.

It has been a year since the final episode of *A Kindred Spirit* aired, and I am now ten. With the volume turned all the way down so no one (including myself) can hear, I change the channel from Fairchild to channel 39, Showcase. The kitchen is once again illuminated by the neon, psychedelic colours and half-naked, ripped torsos grinding to what is in all likelihood some loud, dancey theme song of *Queer as Folk*.

Queer as Folk also centers on a group of gay and lesbian characters who are a chosen family as opposed to a biological family, living and loving in Pittsburgh. I watch mesmerized as I did before, examining the lifestyles of these people and how they don't change sexual orientations or get killed off. It takes me a while to notice, probably because I am so curious and fascinated by the drama as well as all the skin on screen, that the main cast—and pretty much everyone else—is all white.

But as I tuck my arms inside my T-shirt to keep warm in the freezing kitchen, I am surprised to see an Asian character in tonight's episode. He is Japanese, I think. I lean in closer, waiting to see what will happen to him. The young Asian man kisses an older white man who wears big-framed glasses; then it looks like the main characters somehow figure out he is actually a hustler and only interested in the older man's money, so they shame him. The rest of the episode centers on the main cast as they silently go about doing the usual things: walking around, arguing, kissing, and dancing with other shirtless, buff white men in clubs.

When I creep back to my room and lie down and face the shadows on the wall, I wonder when the Asian man will return.

He never does. Nor does any other Asian character ever appear.

Night after night, I shiver in the light of the TV and return to my room somehow feeling colder than I had when I left it.

Although I am never caught, I stop sneaking around at night. I grow weary of waking up in the middle of the night for this show that makes me sigh in disappointment afterward (plus, I find that I really enjoy continuous, uninterrupted sleep). When I consume gay teen novels like *Rainbow Boys*, *The Geography Club*, and *Boy Meets Boy*, I absolutely love them but can't help but feel a little bummed that the protagonists are always gay white teens or teens without specific ethnicities. I discover *Xtra! West*, the local LGBT newspaper, and read articles written about non-Asian people who also seem to be in all of the photos. Even when I help establish the gay-straight alliance at my high school, a school with an overwhelming majority of Asian students, I find myself the only Asian person in the room during meetings.

Maybe, I reason, *I can't find myself in all these things because freaks like me don't exist. Maybe I never will.*

Years later, I am sitting in yet another meeting for the

gay-straight alliance in high school, where, once again, the hard, plastic, empty seats outnumber human bodies. When I was fourteen, I took the plunge and came out to my close friends, who were all extremely supportive. I haven't looked back since. It is now my senior year, and although I feel a bit more comfortable about myself, I haven't met anyone else like me, which is what I expected after coming out. Perhaps my theory that I am alone is true after all.

For our first meeting of the year, Allysha, the president/leader of the group, suggests we watch the TV movie about Marc Hall, the teenager who wanted to bring his boyfriend to the prom hosted by his Catholic high school. The other two attendees in the room, like me, shrug and Allysha takes this as consent. She pops in the DVD and we turn off the lights.

Ten minutes into the film, the classroom door opens. A hefty shadow, backlit by the incandescent hallway light, blocks the door. The near-falsetto pitch of the voice and its obvious gayness surprise me.

"What are you doing?" the shadow asks.

The room is illuminated again and Allysha pauses the film with the remote. She turns to us. "This is Jacky. He's going to be helping me lead the club and then take it over next year." She turns her attention back to Jacky, and in a softer, almost apologetic tone, she explains, "We're just watching a movie."

Now that the lights are on, I get a good look at him. Jacky wears a striped polo shirt that is probably a large or x-large; his cheeks are big and round, and his hair similarly alternates between streaks of black and blonde. He's certainly not modeled after the men on *Queer as Folk,* that's for sure. But it's something more obvious about him that makes me stare.

Jacky is Asian. And as I learn later, he is Chinese. Like me.

"What are you guys doing?" Jacky repeats in his high voice. "There's so much work to do."

I look at Allysha, who wordlessly turns off the TV as Jacky walks past her and pulls out a folder from his bag, ready to get down to business.

That night, when I get home, I flip through my yearbook and discover that Jacky is two years younger. He seems happy in his picture.

I wonder how that can be.

Later that week, at the usual 6pm rehearsal for Chamber Choir class, I glance around the room at both familiar and new faces. And of course, I see Jacky, sitting and chatting with some of the altos. I take my place at the end of the semicircle with the other basses, and when Ms. Comfort arrives, I expect Jacky to slide down a few seats to join the tenor section.

But he doesn't. Something must be wrong.

Ms. Comfort commands everyone to stand up and we run through some warmups. Out of the corner of my eye, I spot Jacky standing next to my sister, his mouth open and smiling. His clear falsetto drifting around the room.

I expect names. I expect taunts. I expect insults.

None of those things happen, not even from the guys. Jacky is clearly gay—if his voice isn't enough of a giveaway, then his roaring laugh combined with a tail-end squeal should—and yet he never gets stabbed or pushed out of a window at school, doesn't show any signs of magically switching teams. English is his first language, and he doesn't seem interested in sleeping with older white men for money. *Who is this guy?* I find myself wondering. Like when I first encountered Jackie and Gary, I am puzzled by his existence.

During the break, I go for a walk down the faded brown hallway floors. When I return to the chatter-filled room, I see Jacky sitting between the altos and sopranos, conversing amiably with some of the girls. I study their faces, but don't see any trace of confusion, disgust, or discomfort; they are all grinning, hanging on Jacky's every word as he tells a story.

And that's when I figure him out.

Jacky belongs on neither channel. Like me, he just is. Seeing him so happy, he seems as natural and comfortable as ever.

And maybe, I think as I watch him, *there are more than just two channels out there.*

Maybe I can be my own channel. A channel featuring a guy who is equal parts Chinese, Canadian, and gay, who can stand up straight and stare into the camera instead of looking to the sides to see if he is correctly being himself or shrinking away because he is different.

That's something I'd like to see, I muse. I hear Jacky give his signature roar-squeal, and it makes me smile.

IDENTITIES

WHEN my short film, *Stay*, was scheduled to screen at the Vancouver Queer Film Festival in 2010, I received an email from a local gay publication asking me to do an interview. Naturally, I was excited (I love talking about myself, but don't get to do it much in person).

One interview question stood out: "When you add your sexuality to the mix, what unique obstacles do you as a gay man of colour have to deal with?"

Although the reporter asked about being a gay man of colour, I felt the answer couldn't be confined to only two layers of my identity. Because it would be one thing to be queer in China or Hong Kong (where my father and mother are from, respectively), but it's another set of difficulties in Vancouver. At the same time, the question touched on the perpetual crisis of identity prevalent in Canada (and particularly Canadian literature, it seems; an English professor in college once half-joked that Canadian writing is either about identity or incest).

His question should really have been this: When you add your sexuality to the mix, what unique obstacles do you as a gay man of colour have to deal with specifically in Canada?

Answering this question is not easy. To begin, I would have to go back to how I identify myself, which I have never really given much thought about. I am aware of all the different pieces that my hybrid identity consists of, but how much I identify with each of them and how that plays into what I call myself had not crossed my mind. Perhaps it was time I examined myself more closely.

I am reminded of an instance when working as a writing tutor on campus at the University of British Columbia. Most of my colleagues were also coincidentally Asian and Canadian.

"Would you say you identify as Chinese-Canadian, or Canadian, or something else?" one of them asked me one afternoon. I mentally clothed myself in both terms, seeing which fit me and felt most comfortable to wear.

"Canadian, for sure."

Their surprised faces met mine. "Why? Don't you feel like you're leaving out the fact that you're Chinese?"

"Why do I have to add my ethnicity to my nationality? I feel like being Chinese is encompassed in saying I'm Canadian. Calling myself Canadian doesn't mean I'm not Chinese. We're a diverse country, right?"

They nodded, considering it. "That's an interesting way of looking at it."

I didn't think it was particularly interesting, but then again, it's a subconscious process, how one chooses to identify themselves. I have certainly called myself Chinese-Canadian on countless occasions and at some point, I must have stopped to analyze what it truly meant to label myself as such, subconsciously or otherwise.

I was born in Canada. I didn't immigrate here when I was a child, so I don't hesitate to claim my nationality as Canadian. There is no doubt there.

The tricky part is whether or not to tie ethnicity with nationality—and also why or why not. We North Americans like to hyphenate our nationalities. African-American. Korean-American. I feel like most of the time, we do this out of reflex, because it is more common than simply using your ethnicity or nationality alone to describe you. I wonder if one of the reasons people of colour do this is because it serves as a quick, convenient label to halt any possible interrogation from those who frequently question others' ancestry (in my life, these inquirers have mostly been white people).

I can certainly see the merits of using a hyphenated descriptor. It presents both your ethnicity and your nationality in one. A package deal. At the same time, I can't help but feel like by telling people I am Chinese-Canadian, I am implying that my two identities are mutually exclusive. If I tell people I am Chinese, they may believe I was born in China or Hong Kong. This isn't necessarily a bad thing, but I feel as though people make certain assumptions about me, such as my language skills and upbringing. And at the same time, I declare myself as simply Canadian and my friends and colleagues look at me funny, expecting my ethnicity in there somewhere too. Neither of these is who I really am.

It is this mentality that bothers me. It is as if I must be ethnically white to be able to use the lone descriptor of Canadian, which I don't believe at all. No one labels themselves as Caucasian-Canadian; less often, we see or hear terms such as German-Canadian or Irish-American or Australian-American. Though some people use them, I cannot help but think that sometimes white people just round up their nationality

to Canadian because all the other white people do it too—
and because no one bats an eye when they do so. Of course,
I acknowledge that part of this may just be a generalization
and sure, maybe I have a secret mission to get back at white
people for racism and colonialism and the atrocity to human
ears known as EDM.

But even when, for instance, I'm on the bus or the SkyTrain and I hear Caucasian people around me speaking in
Irish, English, Australian accents who mention having lived
in Canada for a few months or a few years, or even when
they don't mention it at all, I can't help but feel like other
Canadians—and really, the rest of the world—would consider
them to be more typically "Canadian" simply due to their skin
colour than me, despite the fact that I have only ever lived in
one country my entire life. I know this thinking is wrong, that
I am projecting my thoughts onto and blaming the public,
but it's difficult not to feel like this when I have come across
so many people who have, in turn, made me feel like Canada
is not my home (or the numerous times I have been strolling downtown and someone hands me a flyer for ESL classes,
no doubt assuming I don't speak English well because I am
Asian).

When my sister Maggie visited her friend Anna in Win-
nipeg, a friend of Anna's exclaimed, "Wow, your English is so
good!" My sister simply stared at her, while Anna did a face-
palm. I can't even begin to count the number of times I have
had someone ask me, "Where are you from?"—only to follow
up with "No, where are you *really* from?" or "Where are your
parents from?" when I reply I am from Vancouver.

I fucking hate when this happens to me. It is beyond irritating; it is well within offensive territory. Intentionally or not, whenever this happens, people make me feel like I do not belong and that Canada is not my true home, like it is impossible for them to believe someone who isn't white could be born and raised in Canada. To them, I must be some sort of immigrant and they will not be satisfied with my answer until they have traced back my ancestral migration route to a country far away enough. There is also an air of smugness, of superiority from the inquirer that automatically makes me have a negative impression of them. If people asked about my background more tactfully (for example, "What's your background?" or "What's your ethnicity?") I would have much less of a problem with it. Instead, I end up resenting their ignorance (and I don't like feeling negative! Argh!).

It all came to a head at an incident during a screening at the Vancouver Queer Film Festival. I was seated next to an older, white gentleman. While we waited for the film to begin, he turned to me and made small talk. It started out the way it usually does.

"So where are you from?"

Familiar with how only saying "Vancouver" can be misinterpreted as where I currently reside, I tried my best to be clear. "I was born in Vancouver."

"Ah, I see. I mean, are you from China? Or Hong Kong?"

I bristled at his words. I had just told him where I was from, but I knew what he was really asking.

"My parents are from China and Hong Kong, yes," I said, barely able to keep the equivalent of an eye-roll in my voice.

"Oh, I see." I thought that was the end of it. He had already placed me outside of Canada, making me feel like an outsider, but that was nothing new. I shrugged it off. We returned to staring at ads for local businesses on the screen in silence.

"Where in China are you from?"

Oh my fucking god. I was so angry and exasperated that I was only able to growl through clenched teeth, "I don't know. I'm not from China," and he backed off. It was yet another one of those instances where I apparently could not call myself a Canadian without having to concede that my parents—and by extension, myself—were from elsewhere.

In that moment, I thought back to how I used to joke that the next time someone asked me where I was really from, I would turn the question back on them, just to see how they'd like feeling de-Canadianized. Detecting a vague European accent in the older man's voice, I posed the alienating question to him (with some residual seething in my voice).

Sweden, he told me.

"Where in Sweden are you from?" I inquired, self-satisfied at my pompousness.

He mentioned the name, somewhere outside of Stockholm. He landed in Canada when he was seventeen.

Unfortunately for me, he didn't seem at all bothered by me trying to place him away from Canada, perhaps because he actually grew up in another country. It also likely had to do with him being white and thus unaccustomed to racism and its nuances. But maybe he was nonchalant because he didn't care what a stranger thought of him and felt assured enough to call himself a Canadian regardless. I had tried to highlight a double standard and make someone feel like an outsider the way I constantly felt, but I failed. At the very least, I hoped mirroring the question would inspire empathy and understanding but instead, it seemingly did nothing. Mostly, I felt disappointed at the injustice of it all.

What does a Canadian look like? Everyone will give you different answers. I remember watching the opening ceremonies of the 2010 Winter Olympics on television. Sure, the games were set in Vancouver, but judging by the entertainment in the ceremonies, it was a broader, Canadian theme: the RCMP, a giant spirit bear puppet, Indigenous peoples, and fiddlers representing the Maritimes. It was all spectacular and impressive, but something felt lacking. My best friend Chelsea summed it up best when she lamented, "I know it's kind of mean to say this… but they're the Vancouver games! They're our games, so they should be about Vancouver. We shouldn't have to represent all of Canada. I don't care about fiddlers!"

I think what she was driving at was that fiddlers are cool, but you would be hard-pressed to find any in Vancouver. With visible minorities comprising more than fifty percent of Metro Vancouver's population, and given the important role the Chinese, among other minorities, played in the history of Canada, it was disappointing (but not altogether surprising) that neither the opening nor closing ceremonies included anything that truly reflected Canada's multiculturalism. I didn't see myself there. We didn't see ourselves as Canadians.

The history of Chinese in Canada can be traced back to

the 18th century—and possibly earlier—even before the in-flux of workers who toiled away on the national railway. The Chinese were largely viewed as "others" and job stealers by the white Canadians; segregated from the rest of society, the Chinese built their own Chinatowns. Despite the fact that Chinese families have lived in the country for generations, many Canadians continue to believe they are not true citizens. Colonialism, in all its glory.

And this borderline xenophobia goes both ways. Grow-ing up, my mom used to tell me, "Don't forget that you are Chinese first, above all else"—"all else" meaning Canadian. I have tried to explain my nationality to her, to remind her that until I was twenty-three, I had never set foot in either China or Hong Kong (or Asia, for that matter). She simply waved me off.

To my mom and likely other hyphenated citizens, it doesn't matter where you are born. Ethnicity trumps all.

I have had customer-service jobs where people approach me and start speaking in Cantonese or Mandarin. Although I try my best to converse, I almost always resort to Chinglish—easy words in Cantonese, everything else filled in in English, in the vain hope that they will understand. Depending on the complexity of their question, most of the time they get a vague idea of what I attempt to convey. At least people are un-derstanding about my rudimentary language skills; once they hear me struggling with the language, they ask if I was born in Vancouver. When I tell them yes, they usually say, "Ahh" and nod, and I can't help but feel like I have let them—and my culture—down.

When I tell my mom of my embarrassing run-ins, she clicks her tongue at me. "That is why you should have stayed in Chinese school. More and more people are speaking Chinese these days. I keep telling you how it is an important skill to have." Many times, I have pointed out the fact that we live in Canada, where fluency in English is more important (as evidenced by me frequently helping her spell words to be written on cheques and sick letters, but the irony is lost on her).

Comedian Margaret Cho jokes about her childhood, "It's hard when you're a child of immigrants. You spend half of your day in America, and the rest of your day in a *foreign land*," emphasizing the last two words as if it is an exotic and magical realm.

When I was a teenager, I often slashed the pages of my journal with a pen, venting about my mother, "I feel like I'm living with someone from China!" She didn't understand or speak English very well, and mostly communicated with me in Cantonese. Getting good grades and studying were her highest priority, and were enforced. She yelled at me if I didn't practice piano; if I went out, I had to basically give her full disclosure of who, what, where, when, how, why. Sometimes, I was cognizant enough to see that we are simply two very different people living in different societies in different times. However, this realization only served to make me feel the distance from my family and my culture, instead of reconciling us.

I have met other Chinese-Canadians who nonchalantly toss out, "Oh, you're a banana too, eh?" or "I'm pretty much white-washed too." To me, both "banana" and "white-washed" have negative connotations, as if I am rid of any and all Chinese culture aside from my skin. At first, I wholly rejected this term. The concept of being yellow on the outside and white on the inside makes it sound as if I am a white person in yellow-face and Chinese drag. It seems so odd to me to claim such a thing, but I realize I am speaking from the experience of being a first-generation Canadian to parents who were born and lived in Asia.

On second thought, is that not who I essentially am? I am an atheist compared to my Buddhist mother; I don't really follow the Lunar Calendar and I'm certainly not as traditional as my parents. The only things Chinese about me are my skin, the fact that I eat Chinese food, and my recollection of a moderate amount of Chinese vocabulary and phrases. I'm into classic movies, Sarah McLachlan, and Internet access for all. Seems pretty non-Chinese to me.

Oh, and I am gay too.

For the most part, being gay and Canadian isn't really a point of contention (except maybe if you live in Alberta). Yes, there are still issues here and there, like in 2006 when Stephen Harper held a vote in Parliament to re-address same-sex marriage even after it had been legalized.

It would be naïve to believe that you can be out and queer all across Canada, regardless of where you go. There are still gay-bashings; homophobia and transphobia continue to linger, and will probably do so for decades to come. For the most part though, I felt like it was okay to be gay growing up. The Vancouver Public Library had lots of queer material about and for teens; I discovered and attended a gay youth drop-in. Although my high school had a gay-straight alliance, the rest of the school seemed fairly indifferent to it. When I came out to my aunt at fourteen, she advised me not to tell my class-mates because teens were bullied and sometimes killed due to their sexual orientation. I remember disbelieving her warn-ing because she lived in the US and didn't understand that things weren't the same in Canada. At the time, I was all too familiar with gay teens getting assaulted and harassed (from the many young-adult gay-themed novels I read, not having experienced it firsthand), but I never believed that people at my high school were homophobic enough to enact violence. Sure, I heard people say homophobic shit every day, but it was so casual that it suggested stupidity and ignorance rather than a broken jaw.

My mom once casually mentioned, "Everyone has a sick-ness. Your sister's sickness is that she stays out too much and too late."

"And mine?" I asked, not taking her seriously.

"Yours is you are gay."

And the sad thing is that I knew she genuinely believed it.

***

It might be obvious, but the part of me that struggled with homosexuality was my Chinese side.

"How can you be gay? No one in our entire family is gay," both my father and mother told me when I came out to them in my teens. I'm pretty sure that although it would appear that no one in our current extended family is gay, it doesn't mean they aren't. (Just because someone marries someone of the opposite sex doesn't mean they're straight. I have a specific relative in mind who may be gay but I probably shouldn't mention who they are). It also doesn't mean that no one in the entire lineage of Chans in the history of the world has ever had a homosexual experience.

Needless to say, being Chinese and gay has been, and continues to be, a battle. In Chinese culture, it is a taboo subject. And because so few Chinese gay men (and possibly women too) come out, there is little discussion, education, and understanding around it. Chinese people are supposed to get married and have kids, to pass on the family name. It is not Chinese to be gay.

In the months and years after I came out to my mother, I forced myself to tell her about the dates I went on, queer events I attended, and relationships I was in. For the most part, my mom said nothing, or, if she said anything, there was a long pause, followed by something along the lines of, "Don't get into that stuff right now. Just concentrate on school." Conversations were so awkward, so stilted and unnatural that I wondered if it was worth it to keep bringing up my sexuality with my mom, making both of us so uncomfortable that we avoided speaking to each other the rest of the day.

Even as China and Hong Kong become more modern and open, older generations remain traditional. My dad claimed being gay wasn't natural. My mother advised me never to tell my grandparents because she said they would not understand and that it would hurt them. I have met dozens of gay Chinese men who are in the closet, some firmly (and happily) so. When I tell them I'm out to my Chinese family and have been since I was a teenager, they look at me wide-eyed as if stunned I am alive to tell the tale, then ask me how it happened.

Let me say this: I am proud to be gay and Chinese. It might be a strange thing to be proud of, and it's a little complicated to explain. Part of it is having the courage to defy what others and the heterosexist culture you grew up in want you to be in order to be yourself. If it is true that none of my ancestors were openly gay, then I have broken tradition, broken taboo.

In a wider context, although it may be unfair to compare myself to other gay Chinese men for the sake of feeling proud and superior, it does make me feel somewhat special to know that I can come out to my parents, my friends, and my work, and lead an honest life while some of them remain afraid to live the lives they truly want. Of course, I wish they could join me and live freely too. I have tried to explain to them that coming out is not as bad as they make it seem, but fear paralyzes them, sadly.

A few years ago, there was controversy when a group called Parents' Voice opposed an anti-homophobia policy proposed by the Burnaby School Board. The parents consisted mostly of immigrant families—more specifically, religious Asian parents. They alleged that the policy protected queer kids but not everyone else from bullying; they later added that the policy would force their kids to take sex education classes and learn about homosexuality. Despite accusations of being homophobic, they insisted they were not, that it was not the issue.

When the story broke, I couldn't help but feel like I knew exactly what these parents were doing. On the surface, they tried to appear reasonable, their concerns legitimate. It was the classic Chinese thing to do. But whenever they spoke of their children, all I heard was, *"I don't want my child to be around gay things because I am threatened by them."* Whenever they mentioned how they were not homophobic, I translated it to, *"I'm very homophobic. I was taught that gayness is a terrible thing. Teaching my kids that it is acceptable is wrong."*

When they claimed that news media did not understand their culture and background, I wanted to shout, "Well, I am gay and Chinese, so I do understand. And I think this is clearly about you, so stop hiding behind your kids—who, by the way, already know about and accept gay people. Sorry. Someone had to break it to you."

Once again, it seemed like there was a clear divide: there are gay people, and then there are straight Chinese people. No in-between.

I think this discrepancy can be explained quite simply: if no one speaks about homosexuality and no one is out, then of course it seems like being gay is nonexistent in Chinese culture. And furthermore, which depictions of queers have they likely seen? All those white celebrities living in those Western countries where men can marry men and women marry women and everyone basically walks down the street in their underwear and assless chaps for all to see. In such a conservative society, it is no wonder older Chinese generations misunderstand and disapprove.

Not that the gay community is super accepting of Chinese queers either. Which is not to say it's completely unwelcoming; I have always walked down Vancouver's Davie Street without incident. The few times I have gone out to the Pumpjack Pub or to other gay clubs or bars have been uneventful (too uneventful, I'd say. What do I have to do to get a handsome stranger to say hi and buy me a drink?).

But when you think of the gay community and its members, who do you picture? Perhaps hairless young twinks in clubs and burly bears in leather bars; whatever the hell otters are; older men who lived through the HIV/AIDS era; topless butch and femme women on motorcycles at the Dyke March; trans activists. How many of those people did you imagine were white? How many were of colour?

When the Burnaby School Board was in the news, the policy's supporters were slinging their own hate. "Say goodbye to your businesses, you Asian pricks, you will be run out of town. We will protest your stay in Canada and your fucking corner shops. Goodbye!" someone posted in response to one of *Xtra! West*'s articles.

As awful as that comment is, in their defence, this sentiment and others like it was directed at the older, ignorant demographic that many considered unreasonable and illogical, not necessarily at those like me. But a racist statement is still a racist statement; ignorance fighting ignorance is still feeble. I also don't find it fair to attribute homophobia to an entire race. Fred Phelps, of the infamously homophobic Westboro Baptist Church, is white, but we don't consider all old white people to be hateful.

Another reader noted, "I don't understand why I have to put up with people coming into Canada and trying to change our progressive country/city because they're ignorant." Is it bad that I can understand this point of view and support it? I don't want our hard-earned rights eroded away because people come to live here and don't agree with what has been established. Yet, I can't help but feel guilty for thinking this, as if I am letting down current as well as prospective immigrants, who may share the experience with me of being minorities from similar cultures. And the Canadian part of me says we should accept them and their beliefs because freedom of opinion is one of the fundamental freedoms enshrined in our charter and guaranteed to all Canadians, even if I disagree with their views. That's part of what makes our country great.

Who do I listen to? Who is right? And if I choose one and not the others, does that mean I can no longer identify as such?

Sometimes I feel like I have three identities and each one expects me to pledge allegiance to its side: are you Chinese or Canadian? Are you gay or Chinese? Which one will it be? Choose carefully or you will not be invited back.

For years, it eluded me what to call myself. It took me a while to realize that despite these identities being disparate slices of a pie, they all had one thing in common: me. I have a choice in how I present myself. Who says that if I'm going to label myself as Chinese, I have to speak fluent Cantonese and adopt traditional Chinese customs? Who made it mandatory to denounce minorities for being intolerant in order to be gay? The answer to both seems to be the vague "they" of society—or another way of looking at it: no one in particular.

This whole quandary is like the concept of masculinity. There is no checklist of traits or a test a man must pass in order to call himself "masculine." A giant, 'roided-up guy can say he is masculine, but so can a swishy bleach-blond twink. I believe they would both be right. After all, who would anyone be to say otherwise? There is no masculinity judge who gives you an official stamp if you're masculine enough. It's a subjective term.

Identity functions the same way. I know enough Cantonese, know enough about Chinese culture and customs to be able to comfortably and confidently call myself Chinese. I was born and raised in Canada, one of the best countries in the world, and I am proud that I can think critically about political issues and enjoy the freedoms that I am entitled to. And I am not ashamed to admit that being queer is a significant part of my life.

In fact, I genuinely feel like these three parts share equal space in me. Despite the fact that they shouldn't necessarily get along, they do, at least for me.

Nonetheless, it has not always been a smooth ride. This journey of exploration, as complicated as it has been, has actually made things easier now; even writing this essay has made me more comfortable using Chinese-Canadian to describe myself (though I'd still say I prefer saying Canadian).

With all this in mind, I returned to the original interview question:

"When you add your sexuality to the mix, what unique obstacles do you as a gay man of colour have to deal with?"

I paused for a minute to gather my thoughts, to listen to the three parts of myself and directed their answers:

"Hmm, if you mean unique obstacles I face as a gay Chinese man in life (and not film-related), well, where do I begin? Seriously though, there are always issues with the two, or at least with me. Despite having raised their children in Canada, my parents are traditional Chinese people, which, as I'm sure you can imagine, already brings up problems. It was difficult to come out to them because I never felt like they understood what it was like to be gay or even the concept of it. The whole subject of being gay is a taboo in Chinese culture, so if no one talks about it, how could they understand it, let alone me? And I guess more unique to me, I feel like I am a different breed of gay Chinese man—and not necessarily in a good way. I think some people look at me and dismiss me as a typical gay Asian man but for one, I'm completely out, which a lot of Asian men aren't. I've lived here all my life, and though English is my first language, I don't consider myself white-washed; and I'm not particularly into the 'gay scene' (i.e. clubbing, going to bars and big parties, etc.).

"I'm a strange mashup of Chinese, Canadian, and gay, where I feel like there's a balance of all three."

THE ONE IN TEN

"I wrote a poem for someone. I don't think, um... uh... he knows though."

While at work with no one around, I came out to my friends and co-workers. Without missing a beat, Lisa and Yilin both inquired, "Oooh, who?" with arched eyebrows and mischievous grins on their curious faces.

"Someone in my poetry class."

"Oh, interesting," mused Yilin. She was a fellow undergrad in the Creative Writing Program at UBC and was especially intrigued, since we were in the same poetry class and she had read my poem (which I had completely forgotten about). "So, who is it?"

"Well, there aren't exactly a lot of guys in the class, so that kinda narrows it down. Come to think of it, there aren't a lot of guys in the program," I noted. Yilin paused for a second before agreeing. To Lisa's entertainment and exclusion, Yilin and I started naming all the guys in our Creative Writing courses while I tried to keep track of the number on my fingers—which inevitably led to confusion. We were so disorganized, I finally stood up and jotted their names on the whiteboard behind us. When we were done, ten names were written in blue. While Yilin and Lisa contemplated the board, I came to a realization.

They say there is one gay person for every ten.

I looked at the board, and then at my name at the top of the list of nine others.

***

"Everybody's gay these days," straight people joke. It is safe to say that most people know at least one person who is gay; a 2012 survey conducted by Forum Research found that eight in ten Canadians say they know someone who is LGBT. I never really believed everyone was gay, and I didn't think it was particularly funny. If everyone was gay, where were all of them and why did I only keep meeting straight people?

Vancouver is a mid-sized port city that has, since the 1980s, received a significant number of immigrants from all over the world. Furthermore, Canada also grants asylum to those fleeing oppressive, violent societies, promising safety and fresh beginnings; people from diverse cultures, backgrounds, ages, ethnicities, and life experiences add more tiles to the heralded mosaic of Canadian society. The Vancouver Pride Parade is one of the largest in the country. Gay-straight alliances have been providing safe zones for students in most high schools, universities, and colleges for years. Various hate-crime laws in the province are designed to combat homophobia and to make citizens feel comfortable being themselves. All this should mean queer people are everywhere, out and visible.

I have worked at an electronics store (Future Shop), a cinema (Fifth Avenue Cinemas), a public garden (Van Dusen Botanical Gardens), and on campus (UBC). Since my teens, I have volunteered at several organizations and events. Occasionally, I will attend birthday parties as well as dinners with my large extended family of aunts, uncles, and cousins. Other times, my best friend Chelsea will end up dragging me out to random outings around town. But no matter where I go and whoever surrounds me, I often feel like—and am—the only gay person. The one in ten.

Perhaps I am just being overly self-conscious when I move about in these different spaces. As a gay man of colour, I can't help but be aware of my presence and observe how others will react and behave whenever I enter a room (sometimes I am more aware than other times, like when I'm in a predominantly white crowd). Or perhaps attentiveness is merely a subconscious process of trying to identify other potential queer bodies around as possible love interests, or a safety mechanism to determine if the group one is around won't beat the crap out of them.

The one in ten theory was developed by Alfred Kinsey and has, since the 1940s, become a hard-and-fast rule for estimating the gay population. I don't recall where I first heard it, but I came across the stat numerous times in the pages of gay-themed YA novels during my early teens as I was working my way up to coming out. In those stories, characters besides the protagonist—the crush, the quiet kid, the macho football jock—were also, much to their shock, gay as well. The more stories I read about queer teens as average kids amongst the masses, the more I believed that they, too, must be roaming the hallways at my school, chameleons camouflaging with the straights. And if high school were just a microcosm of society, then it followed that gay men and women were everywhere:

the guy walking down the street with blaring headphones on, the woman in a business suit on her way to her shitty marketing job. They were all secretly there.

Perceptions are powerful things. They inform your worldview, and can be difficult to alter once firmly established. But things that are incorrectly perceived can also lead to an incorrect belief. For instance, a bent-looking pencil in water might make you believe all pencils in water bend, or that pencils are capable of bending. Sometimes the perceived reality is accurate, but other times, it is misinformed. Then it becomes an illusion.

For me, I began to think that maybe there were more gay people around me than I knew. When I loitered in the mall or traveled on buses to and from school, I used to smile at guys I thought were cute. If they noticed me—they almost never did—they usually stared back, probably wondering what the hell this random kid was doing, creepily leering at them. And although nothing more ever happened, I used to beat myself up for letting slip the chance to flirt with cute boys (not that I even had the guts to say hi to a stranger, let alone flirt with someone).

Case in point: it was Friday night at a bowling alley. The air in the room was filled with the aroma of greasy pizza and the crashing dull thuds of balls striking the wooden floor. To my astonishment, I was in the lead in my lane, ahead of Chelsea and the rest of her Science Co-Op colleagues from university (at which I wouldn't study at for another few years; I was still a student at Langara College). Yet another event Chelsea had wrangled me into attending.

I watched Kevin as he picked up a ball, tested it in his palm. He was wearing forest-green chinos and a t-shirt over a long-sleeve. He shuffled down to the line, his right leg smoothly gliding and extending behind his left like a pro bowler (or so it seemed to me, at least). When he turned around after only knocking two pins into the back, his face scrunched up in a sour "Aww, fuck" expression-grin. I liked it. I thought he was my kinda guy: handsome but not in a douchey way; stylish but down-to-earth; and him being Asian would make things easier for us to connect over.

Kevin and I chatted sporadically throughout the night, mostly making small talk. I told him I was into writing; he told me he was into biochemistry. After I won the game, I accompanied Chelsea to the concession to get an iced tea.

"So... Kevin's cute," I ventured. A knowing smirk crept across her face; she had heard this before.

"Yeah, he is. You should ask him out!"

I scoffed. "Ha. No." Yet I had already been considering it. I just didn't know how. I spent the rest of the evening brainstorming terrible, clichéd pick-up lines.

At the end of the night, everyone went their separate ways. Much to my chagrin, Kevin hitched a ride with one of the other guys, leaving me and Chelsea to return together. I hadn't mustered enough courage to ask him out. I was disappointed in myself. My only hope was that our paths would somehow cross again, and maybe then, I would be able to do something, but who knew if that would happen.

When my bus arrived, I made for the back where it was empty, and pulled out *Watchmen* from my bag. I got so focused on the story and was so oblivious to what was happening around me that as the bus drove off, I was surprised by a finger inserting itself in the drawn panels on the page. The finger tapped the page twice. I looked up, and lo and behold, it was Kevin. What were the chances? Our meet-cute was straight out of a gay teen book.

I was excited to see him again (but consciously tried not to make it obvious). He sat down beside me and told me his friend had dropped him off at the bus stop since this friend lived further west. We conversed about *Watchmen* and books and movies; it was all surprisingly easy with him, rare when I met people.

As the bus neared my stop, the voice in my head urged me to do something, that there was a reason I had been given a second chance. Because this—seeing the same cute guy twice in the same night—never happened to me.

But I was terrified. And it didn't help that there were witnesses around who would surely point and cackle with laughter when they watched me fail.

I took a breath. With my heart pounding, I asked, "Do you... want to go out, sometime?" I could not believe I even possessed the ability to structure that kind of sentence.

To my surprise, Kevin laughed a little, then stopped when he realized I was not laughing along. "Oh, um, no. No. Sorry."

The bus pulled over. I got up to leave, grateful for my good timing and the convenient exit. "No, no. That's okay." We awkwardly told each other we would talk later, but we both knew it was a lie.

From the bowling alley to the bus, I had never even considered the possibility that Kevin might be something other than gay. In fact, I hadn't thought of him as gay or straight or having any sort of sexual orientation at all, only that he would be into me because the narratives say that gays, in all their normalness, are everywhere—especially when they're cute *and* you bump into them twice in one day. It never occurred to me that the books could be wrong. After all, books are based off reality, right?

When I told Chelsea what happened, she suggested, "Maybe next time you should see if he's gay first." The thought never crossed my mind. I felt foolish, humiliated, and let down, questioning what I deemed to be trustworthy sources and considering for the first time, whether the world wasn't as congruous with fiction as I had believed.

Then again, perhaps encountering others like you is simply a matter of luck. My friend Matt told me how he was sitting at a bar once when this random hot guy chatted him up and ultimately asked him out at the end of the night. I knew someone who told me about how a supposedly homophobic classmate slept over at his place one night and in the morning, they had sex. Both these incidents sound like they belong on the shelves with the novels where gays are abundant and loneliness is short-lived.

Yet, for me, the closest thing resembling a chance meeting like that occurred during a high school music trip in the UK. Following a day of performances, we were scheduled to relax and enjoy ourselves at a dance, sharing the space with another choir from Canada that was also touring the country. While my bandmates "danced" awkwardly to Usher and Britney, I sat by myself at a table in the company of everyone's purses and bags, silently judging how badly teenagers flailed to the aforementioned noise pollution.

"Hey. How are you?" A tall, lanky guy, sporting the sprouts of a moustache, was standing beside me. As we yell-chatted over the noise, I learned Jeremy was in the choir from Mississauga and in his senior year in high school. After a while of conversing, my curiosity finally got the better of me.

"Why did you come talk to me?

He shrugged. "I just had this feeling that I should say hi." If this wasn't an indication that he was gay and into me, I didn't know what was. I mean, our encounter was clearly the beginning of a rom-com. When I returned to my room that night, the first line I wrote in my journal was "I think I found the guy from my stories." Why else would a dude randomly start talking with another dude if he wasn't gay?

Jeremy and I kept in touch via email when we returned to Canada, and after some hesitation, I finally came out to him. I wasn't sure how he would react, but I certainly didn't expect him to tell me he was a Christian, the kind that believed in "hate the sin, not the sinner." Suddenly, what once seemed like destiny now appeared to be a prank. Needless to say, we eventually lost touch (aside from an instance of him accidentally adding my address to an email urging his friends to rally against gay marriage before it was inevitably legalized. He then personally apologized for his mistake in a second email).

The stories I grew up reading and watching—these narratives seem to exist and occur, but not to me. Gay people might indeed be everywhere, and these narratives are waiting to happen—if only these people were noticed.

One of the most useful and advantageous things about being gay is possessing a gaydar so you can locate other gay people around you for friendship or fucking or whatever.

I do not have a gaydar.

I wish I did, but for the life of me, I do not. I will say what little I do possess has improved over the years, but I continue to find it difficult to be certain unless the guy has a high-pitched voice and uses the word "fierce" (and even then I still doubt myself); part of it is that I do not want to rely on stereotypes or assume anyone is anything without knowing for certain, which equates to the world appearing to be one gigantic heterosexual machine to me. My gaydar has been so terrible that during my time in film school, I came up with an original TV pilot about a guy whose friends set him up on dates to develop and improve the gaydar that he lacks. I called it *No Signal.*

During the summer, our class was assigned to collaborate with acting students for a week to write and arrange an original show. This was my first project working with actors, or pretty much anyone outside of the writing program itself. When we met the actors, I didn't think much of them; they were always spontaneously breaking out into songs, roaring with laughter, or shouting amongst themselves (as I learned most actors do).

One afternoon, in the classroom that had basically become our second home for the week, my writer classmates and I took a break to relieve our mental processes by, of course, gossiping.

"Did you know there's some drama between the actors?" Rachel shared. "Kieran, Natasha's roommate, doesn't like Matt. See, Matt's dating this guy—"

"*What*?" I was dumbfounded, to put it mildly. I hadn't the slightest inkling that any of the actors were gay, least of all Matt.

"Yeah," continued Rachel, "and this guy is someone Kieran was interested in but never made a move to ask out."

"WHAT?"

Everyone laughed. "No signal?" quipped Joe, referencing my TV show. Here were two guys, Matt and Kieran, both gay, and I had no clue, despite seeing them every single day that week. If I didn't detect them, could other Matts and Kierans be around me too? Could my isolation be at the mercy of my nonexistent gaydar?

And as if picking up a gay signal isn't difficult enough, some gay people are self-proclaimed and proudly "straight-acting," an obnoxious term describing a gay person who believes they pass as a typical heterosexual man but identifies as gay. Personally, I loathe the word because it is loaded with homophobia and femmephobia; lots of men who claim they are "straight-acting" almost brag about it—they say it as a defense, because being gay, to them, is associated with being feminine, which is apparently the most awful thing a gay guy can be (and if you "act" straight, does that mean underneath the so-called "masculine" façade, there's a little queer boy who has watched every season of *RuPaul's Drag Race* and has strong opinions about dresses worn at the Oscars?). But that's a whole other rant. Point is, my fellow gays may be intentionally deceiving everyone including me, making me feel more alone than I truly am.

Alternatively, if gay people appear straight to me, perhaps I come off as heterosexual to them—leading them to not make themselves known to me. I have been told by some that they didn't have the remotest idea I was gay when they met me, while others have informed me (usually with a chuckle) that it is quite obvious. I have heard of the difficulties of appearing stereotypically gay—bullying, teasing—but never the hardships of seeming straight. I wonder if it is a legitimate struggle.

I'm not sure what to think. Some gay guys might be in the same predicament and not possess a functional gaydar. Others, for all I know, might be able to tell that I am gay but choose not to talk to me, for whatever reason. Who knows.

Or could the rooms I enter—classes, workplaces, social settings—attract a straight crowd—and also me? While I studied at film school, the majority of my classmates were male and almost all were straight, including one trans guy. We also had a lesbian in the mix; the three of us were so much more queerness than I had ever experienced, I felt like we could be our own pride parade.

At Langara College, where I took a slew of arts courses, I repeatedly found myself the only man in the class, and likely the only gay one. *Where are all the guys?* I pondered time and time again. Sure, I took a lot of English courses, which I can see isn't a traditionally manly subject. But even when I transferred to the Creative Writing program at the University of British Columbia, I thought for sure there would be more men, since there are so many male writers, and therefore, more gay men. To my dismay, there were not a lot of them in the program, and only one other who openly identified as gay. I met more gay dudes in the business school in university than I did in any other program. Apparently, homos are really into finance and accounting.

Based on profiles and ads on online dating sites, gay men enjoy going to the gym and working out. I prefer exercising my brain by reading books and playing music. Gay people (adults in general, really) sometimes socialize in pubs or bars or go clubbing (though the ubiquity of apps have certainly affected the popularity of these spaces). I rarely drink alcohol; ginger beer or herbal tea at home suits me just fine. The one thing I seem to have in common with other gay men is watching queer films. However, more often than not, I notice that I am one of the youngest in the audience; most everyone else in the forty-and-over demographic and are accompanied by husbands and partners to discuss the films with after the credits have rolled.

Am I alienating myself by not doing the same things that other gay men do? And if so, is modifying who I am the solution?

The possibility makes me wonder how my life would have turned out if I had lived my youth differently.

***

"To the best of your knowledge, how many men who have sex with men, whether they identify as gay or not, do you think

live in the Greater Vancouver Region? Please make an edu-
cated guess as best you can."

I'm sitting comfortably in front of a computer screen in
a cubicle of an office building downtown. About a week ago,
I signed up for a study that will analyze and track the sexual
behaviours and attitudes of men who have sex with men in
and around the city.

I have never really thought about this question before,
and I honestly have no clue, so I try to calculate it instead.
*There's about a million people in Vancouver—I think? No, a bit
more. I think I read somewhere that the total population of Metro
Van is like three million or something? Or maybe it will be soon?
Soon-ish? If it's three million, then ten percent of that is... 300,000.
Wait, what? That's ridiculous. Did I do the math right? Well, I did
almost fail Math 11 and there aren't any calculators around right
now... Fuck, I'll just write 30,000. Even though that seems like
an absurdly high number too.*

I type it in: 30,000. I stare at it for a few moments in
disbelief before I am able to click Next. Can there really be
30,000 gay men and women in Metro Vancouver?

The true demographics on the LGB population are difficult to accurately determine. Many queer people may not
identify as gay or bi for several reasons; certain societies, for
example, continue to persecute queer people (often through
violence or by time in prison), so many keep their sexuality hidden, fearing for their personal safety (and sometimes
for their family and friends' safety too). Some may not even
view themselves as gay or bi, but heterosexual with a casual
hookup with someone of the same sex every now and then.

Others may associate being queer with stereotypes (i.e. feminine men, butch women) that they believe to be negative and hence, refuse to identify as such. Still others might simply not be ready to accept who they are. Whatever the reason, the data is often skewed, even when surveys ask participants to self-report anonymously and guarantee that information will be confidential.

Percentages of the gay population vary within cities and countries. Among the highest is Rio de Janeiro, a city in which, according to a 2009 survey conducted by the University of São Paulo, 14.3% of the men in the city identify as gay or bisexual, a staggering figure that blows my mind into smithereens. In San Francisco, the number is even higher: in 2006, the Williams Institute of the UCLA School of Law found that 15.4% of the city's population say they are gay, lesbian, or bisexual, or 94,234 people. I don't know how to translate these numbers into reality. These percentages seem ludicrous, despite the fact that relative to society as a whole, they are a mere fraction. I can only imagine how living in a city with that many queer people would change the way they live their lives, how they meet people, what they believe, or their perception of the world. Perhaps they have never been the one, but part of the two, three, or four in ten.

However, the overwhelming majority of surveys done worldwide reveal that the numbers are in fact closer to 1-3% of the population. In Canada, Forum Research conducted a telephone survey in 2012 which revealed that 5% of people identify as lesbian, gay, bisexual, or transgender. Based on my experience in Vancouver, this sounds about right, or at least more plausible than ten percent.

All this time, I had been led on by a false hope perpetuated by mainstream media that hordes of gays were roaming the streets. This wasn't the case at all.

When I discover this statistic, a sense of relief, of confirmation, washes over me. But my hopes—and the people with them—have been halved. Because as truth can be enlightening, it can also be sobering.

It is not so much one in ten as it is almost one in a hundred.

The truth validates the part of me that I hoped couldn't be right—that I couldn't truly be as alone as I felt.

It does not matter what the truth is. What matters is what you perceive the truth to be.

If you have always seen the pencil in the water as bent and you are told one day that it is a process called refraction and that the pencil is not actually the way it looks, could you believe it? Or would you continue to believe what appears before your eyes?

I should say that being one in ten isn't a horrible thing (well, depends who the other nine are). For the most part, people are welcoming and don't care if I am gay or not. Some like me more when they find out (which I've always found odd). But it is the feeling of isolation that accrues in you over time and amounts to disappointment and loneliness. Crowd after crowd, the conclusion appears to be the same: you are alone. It is this perception, however incorrect, that becomes your truth. Your life.

We like to reassure youth struggling with their sexuality that they are not alone, that there are many of us in the world who understand because we have similarly struggled but persevered. For queer youth who will similarly struggle to find friends and community as they get older like I do/did, I can see how this lie can be helpful in providing hope versus the alternative ("Guess what? You are as alone as you feel. Once you're legal, visit a gay club or download Grindr and come find the rest of us. Good luck!"). Then again, if I had been told in my teens, or even when I was in college, that the world is a lot less gay that I thought, I'm not sure I would have accepted it. After internalizing all the narratives I had read and watched in films to the point of starring in them myself in my own head, I probably would have felt like a child being told Santa Claus was a fabricated tale when it was the thing keeping me on my very best behaviour every day. Who wants to believe that they are more alone than they think?

On the other hand, giving up completely should not be the answer either. That wouldn't be a hopeful message to send not just to youth, but to adults searching for connection in a big, bad, cold world. The average person doesn't seem to place importance in finding others in public spaces (at least in Vancouver, where we all seem to view each other with distrust and suspicion that often borders paranoia). When my friend Brian asked me once, "Why do you try so hard?", maybe he had a point. Maybe it is better to try less, given the (absence of) results I have yielded thus far. It seems like LGBT people of all ages must deal with loneliness at some point in their lives. Perhaps some of us just have to get used to a little more of it.

So next time when Chelsea recruits me to another event,

perhaps I won't be on the lookout for a fellow black sheep. I suppose I will have to be comfortable in the company of straight people wherever I go (if I'm not on Davie Street), and try not to think about who might be what sexual orientation. I will consider going to a pub. I don't feel like I have much of a choice, unless I want to keep feeling alone. Conform to society or adapt to my solitude.

While riding the bus one overcast afternoon, I open up a recent copy of *Xtra! West* I snagged from a newspaper rack earlier. Someone laments about the dating pool of the city on the editorial page: "With a population at a mere two to four percent, no wonder our choices out there are so slim."

Two to four? Only? Guess that would explain a lot, I think.

As I look up from the paper, I notice a cute guy standing at the back door. He is wearing pressed khakis and a tucked-in dress shirt. In his hand is a protein shake bottle with ice cubes and the milky residue of a smoothie. A brown messenger bag is slung across his chest and hangs by his waist. His hair is neatly coiffed and gelled. As the bus continues, he stares out the front windows, on the lookout for his stop.

I can't help but wish he would look over and catch my eye, but he doesn't. I turn my attention back to the printed words on the page. "Two to four" is all I see now.

When the bus advances towards my stop, I edge myself over to the door. For a brief moment, he glances over at me.

I don't smile at him like I used to. Instead, I push open the door.

Two to four, I remind myself. I get off the bus and walk away without looking back.

The World behind
Closed Doors

I T started the way most Harlequin romance novels do—
via an online dating site.

I was nineteen at the time, and my world was built upon piano keys, all kinds of writing, and crushes on boys who would, one way or another, never end up with me. Now of legal age and more ready than ever to find love, I set out on my search. Because of my lack of a working gaydar, I was resigned to meeting other gay people online (this was back in 2007, when online dating was relatively new and considered by many to be desperate and a bit sketchy). I met Samuel (not his real name) that way, and assumed he was going to be another name added to the list of people I met online who, after meeting them once or twice, I would rather not talk to again. I remember the message he sent me: he mentioned how I said I liked music on my profile, and went on to tell me that he was a student at UBC in the music program. At first, this surprised me—not because he was in the music program, but that someone in cyberspace had 1) bothered to read my profile though it didn't have keywords like "bottom boy," "casual," or the popular misspelling "cum" in it; 2) sent me a message that didn't include the aforementioned words or have the generic "how r u?"; and 3) sent me a message that actually mentioned my interests and started a stimulating conversation. Now this was profound.

We instant-messaged each other for a few days before he insisted we meet sometime soon. Wary of meeting people on-line, I felt rushed. I was used to talking with people on MSN Messenger maybe ten times before seeing them in real life, and here was this guy who seemed anxious to meet after two or three conversations?

To be fair, he wasn't a middle-aged white man who fe-tishized me for being Chinese, which often seemed to be the case. This guy was twenty-one and also Chinese, and it was rare, at least for me, anyway, to meet Chinese or Asian guys who were born in Vancouver and weren't taking ESL classes. Relenting to the pressure, I agreed to meet.

We decided on a Tuesday afternoon after one of my class-es. It was a snowy day in February and since the Vancouver Film School campus was downtown, we decided to meet at a nearby park. I waited under a little gazebo for a while, hoping I wasn't going to get stood up. After a few minutes, he hadn't shown up. I took a walk around the park to see if maybe he was waiting for me elsewhere. The only picture I had of this guy was from his MSN Messenger profile photo: tiny, and a bit grainy. When I spotted a guy down the street who I thought looked like him, I awkwardly walked back to the ga-zebo, following his snowy footprints. When he stood inside the gazebo, waiting, I knew it was him.

Samuel was perpetually tired from early morning class-es, late-night rehearsals, and tutoring; he lived on a diet of whatever fast food was available at the cafeterias on campus as well as home-cooked meals from his mother; and he always wore a blazer like it was a second skin. When I first met him, he gelled his short black hair; on our second date, I casually mentioned that he would look as handsome without the gel. I never saw him with product in his hair again (I was right: he looked better without it). When he let me know he was in the closet, I believed I had read enough gay teen novels to be able to cope with it. After all, how hard could it be? Although I had been out and proud since the age of fourteen, I was an understanding, patient guy and believed he was worth it. A few weeks of dating followed, and Samuel became my first boyfriend.

A couple days later, around midnight, he first came around to my house. He had finished rehearsal at school and was on his way home; he lived a mere five-minute drive away from my place, and could stop by for a bit. The security system beeped fairly loudly when the door to the house was opened. My mom was sleeping and I didn't want to wake her up and have her barge into my room, to discover me with a strange man at midnight. But I was young and instinct-driven, and was willing to risk a confused stare and a lecture in the morning to spend time with my new boyfriend. I told Sam to drop by for a few minutes and though he was even more concerned about my mother's presence than I was, he agreed.

He entered my room hesitantly. We sat on my bed for a few minutes while we filled each other in on our days and the vaguely interesting things that had happened to us. Most importantly, we made out. I knew he had to be home soon since it was late and a short while later, he wished me good-night. As he descended the steps of the porch, I heard my mom's footsteps behind me; she was watching me watching him leave.

"Who was that?" I heard her mumble in her low, sleepy voice.

"Um, a friend."

"Why did you tell him to come here so late? Do you know what time it is? Don't do that again!" And with that she returned to her room, her slippers shuffling on the tiled kitchen floor. When she was gone, I breathed a sigh of relief.

Because Sam was in the closet, I respected his wish not to tell people he was gay. We had difficulty determining whether or not I should tell my mom. I didn't really care, but at the same time, I was unsure if she would allow him to come over anymore. Eventually, we decided it was better she didn't know. I don't remember Sam being afraid of meeting my mom but if I was, my fears were squashed when they finally did meet. Sam scored immediate points when he met my mom while she was awake. It was in the afternoon when he climbed the carpeted stairs in our house. My mom was in the kitchen cooking, surrounded by the steam of bubbling and boiling pots and pans on the stove.

"This is Samuel," I said as he gave her a charming smile.

"Sahhm-yu-al," she repeated slowly, trying to get his name right.

"He goes to school at UBC," I continued. Her face immediately lit up, like hearing one of her kids had taken her advice and was going off to medical school—a look I had never been able to earn from her.

"Ah, really? What are you studying?" she asked in Cantonese, her face practically bursting with enthusiasm. He told her, in Cantonese, that he was in the music program.

"Oh! You know Cantonese!" My mother's voice rose an octave she was so excited.

I headed to my bedroom as my mother's animated voice was telling him how useless I was for choosing to go to film school and not to university to get a proper education while my boyfriend tried to convince her that film school was a good option too. I felt proud that she liked him so quickly, that she approved of him. When asked about how we met, I told my mom he was helping me with my application to the music program at UBC, which if all went well, I would be attending in the fall after graduating from film school later that year. This only made her like him even more (if that was possible). She must have been thinking, *After all my failed nagging, this wonderful guy is helping my son go to university! What a godsend!*

Because of his busy schedule, Sam visited only a couple times a week. During the occasions when my mom was home, he politely greeted her, and she in turn politely asked how school was going and how he was doing. Once, after chatting briefly, Sam came into my room, where we did homework with the door slightly ajar (his suggestion) so my mom didn't get any ideas. In my room, he could be himself. We talked about our next dates and I gave him quick kisses. When my mom went to bed, we quietly had sex, with him being extra-careful I wasn't moaning too loudly.

One of the first times we had sex, he left at around 12:30am. The next morning, when my mother asked me why he had left so late, I replied, "We were playing cards and he fell asleep."

Hanging out with my friends was slightly easier. I told them that Sam was my boyfriend and no one had a problem with it—except Sam. Despite everyone being accepting, he was not comfortable showing affection while we all hung out, keeping his distance while my straight friends and their significant others practically groped one another in front of us. It was as if he were both poles of a magnet: strongly attracted to me only behind my bedroom door, but repelled outside it.

None of his friends knew. We kept up the lie that he was helping me with my university application and nobody questioned it. Every time he introduced me with the line "This is my friend, Aaron," I ignored the tightness in my gut. His friends hovered around him after concerts at school, all of them talking, reminiscing, laughing at teachers and classes, while I shuffled my shoes silently nearby, trying not to feel uncomfortable being labelled just another friend.

While Sam's father was usually away on business in Hong Kong, his mother was suspicious of anyone he had over, even friends. Sam used to say God and suspicion ruled her world, that she was perceptive of people and lies. She was, and likely still is, extremely conservative; Sam once told me that were he to come out to his parents, he truly believed his mom would kill him. Her conservatism made my mother look like Siddhartha Gautama.

Sam's graduation ceremony took place in April; there was a reception in the music building where parents and now graduates took pictures, told each other of future plans, and thanked teachers they had known since freshman year. I somehow found myself standing across from his mother, whom I recognized from earlier when he was taking pictures with his family.

"You must be so proud of him," I said.

She smiled at me, and I wondered if Sam's description of his mother as a follower of the Westboro Baptist Church might be an exaggeration.

"I am. He tried to teach me music but I don't understand it. I just like to listen to it," she replied in Cantonese, chuckling.

Unlike Sam's, my Cantonese is very broken. I can understand it conversationally fairly well but when I speak, it often comes out in fragments. I knew my flawed language skills were not going to impress her.

"That's good," I managed.

There was a brief pause before the expected, yet unexpected, question arose: "How did you two meet? Do you go to school here too?"

Being accustomed to the lie by now, I casually responded, "No, I'm going to film school. Sam's helping me apply to UBC next year."

"Oh. So how did you two meet if you don't go here?"

In that moment, I realized what Sam meant when he told me his mother was perceptive. I saw her glance at my shoulder bag, which had, among other things, a rainbow-silhouetted Mickey Mouse pin and another one that said "Queer" on it. I swallowed hard, uncertain if she was going to bludgeon me with her purse right then and there.

"Ohhh, yeah. I met him through a friend," I mustered,

feigning half a smile. I nodded, as if I was merely clarifying what I meant, while her eyes bore into me. It felt like millennia before she replied.

"Oh. Okay." Her eyes left mine and it appeared I was in the clear.

"Do you think she knows?" I asked Sam one night while we lay in my bed, the lamp on my table illuminating his handsome face.

"I don't know. Do you think *your* mom knows?"

"I don't know."

We certainly were not going to be addressing the issue anytime soon, and like typical Chinese mothers, if they did know, they were not going to say anything either. It was a stalemate.

This went on for weeks; I was introduced as a friend to people in Sam's world, and saw him a few hours a week, if I was lucky. One time, he told me he wished he could stay the night, and that we could sleep together (which inspired me to write and direct my short film *Stay*). When I told him he could, that I didn't care if my mom knew or not, he immediately declined, saying that he couldn't, and I knew he was talking about his family. When we were together, I respected his boundaries and restrained myself from tearing off his clothes and mauling him. I rationalized that although it made me feel shitty to be known as a friend in his life and to not see him as much as I wanted, he was worth it to me. He understood what it was like to be Chinese and gay and strongly supported me in everything that I did in a way I had never gotten from anybody. But gradually, I started to feel that his world was shrinking mine.

I felt more and more like what he was introducing me as: merely a friend.

Sam was over at my place again one evening. He was sitting at my desk, using my computer for homework. My bedroom door was slightly open on his insistence again, and I was on my bed, reading a copy of *Xtra! West*. An ad for the upcoming Pride parade filled the page.

"Are you going to Pride this year?" I thought this was a legitimate question. His face said otherwise: it was a combination of *Are you seriously asking me this?* and *Uh, hell no.* I tried my best to hide my disappointment.

"Okay." What else could I do? I certainly wasn't going to force him to come. But his abrupt dismissal pounded on the door of my mind. After about a minute, I reasoned, "Why not? Lots of straight people go. It doesn't mean everyone there is gay."

But that wasn't safe enough. In his mind, Sam believed that were he to tell his mother that he was going out that day, she would somehow figure out he was going to Pride (as if it were the one and only event happening that day), discover he was gay, and proceed to sharpen her butcher's knife and wait for him to come home with Mardi Gras beads around his neck.

He told me about how his mom had given him everything in his life: support, shelter, love. If he were to come out to her, he believed he would be throwing it all back in her face, that he would be disrespecting her—that he would truly be hurting her. By keeping this secret to himself, he was sparing her the pain.

"What's the worst thing that could happen if you went?"

He sat there, staring at the floor, unable to look at me for several seconds.

"I don't know. I don't have an answer for that. I'm from a different background than you," he mustered, "and my mom is too. I don't expect you to understand."

"I want to understand! You're not giving me answers or explaining so I can't."

We both sat there and avoided each other's gazes. The concept behind the Pride parade is, well, pride. People are able to be themselves and be proud of it. Sam told me that night that he wasn't proud of being gay, of who he is.

Another realization clicked into place. "Wait, so you're never going to come out?" My eyes fixed on him, waiting for a response.

"As long as I'm living in Vancouver, no, I'm not going to come out."

Usually at this point in a story, some clichéd phrase like "my world collapsed at that moment" makes its way onto the page. And though I did feel some devastation, I also had a revelation. All the pieces made sense. I always thought he was worth it, but to be known as a "friend" the rest of our relationship? That didn't make sense. We couldn't do this anymore. What good is a world—a life, a love—if no one can see it?

A few days later, we met again to talk things out. I told him about how I only felt like a friend to him, and that I felt like I was going back in the closet because of it. Every other word from him was "sorry," and though I knew he sincerely meant it, he was unwilling to come out or to change anything. We mutually decided to break up. He tore his world away from the one we had created together, and shut the door.

The Birth and Death of You and Me

I'M sorry I nearly killed you.

You were always more intelligent than me. Before I was born, though you weren't into that Disney shit, the idea of Prince Charming somehow felt so right, like it was what you were made to do. You might have thought it was ridiculous, but you knew you were meant to love.

After coming out to your friends in high school, when they asked what you wanted for your birthday, you always answered, "A boyfriend." They just blinked at you, and you felt like the biggest idiot in the world. Once, when someone on a gay youth networking site sent you a message about how he "would have sex with you if you lived closer," you tried to have a meaningful conversation with him about how sex shouldn't be given up so freely. To your frustration, he didn't seem to comprehend. The entire encounter was so exasperating, you typed up a rant on your Myspace page:

"The person you kiss should mean something. The person you embrace should mean something. The person you do it with should mean something."

People just didn't get it.

When you were almost no longer a teenager, you made finding your prince a near-full-time job. When locating him proved too difficult, what with your underdeveloped social skills and no one returning your glances, you took to the virtual world, rationalizing that there, at least you would know they were gay, which was a start. Older men, sometimes in their forties and usually white, with unusual usernames, flirted with and tried to seduce you—even bluntly told you all the dirty things they wanted to do to you. You simply replied, "Sorry, I don't hook up. Good luck though," and moved on. They were surprised: "Thanks for letting me know at least," they returned. It made you wonder what kind of lost souls were out there.

Then you found him—or rather, he messaged you.

He was around your age, also Chinese, and had a musician's heart. When you were together, you blossomed and blushed. At last, you were able to show your love instead of confining it to pages in a journal and fantasies in your mind. He wasn't out, but that was just a minor detail, you believed. Even though he gave you only a few hours a week, you gave him what you were waiting years to do.

It wasn't enough. One night, he told you that he would never come out to anyone. Being known as a mere "friend" to everyone he knew wore down on you. Within a few months, things fell apart. When he left, he took pieces of you, leaving gaps here and there, like a moth-eaten sweater.

For some reason, you had never thought of the possibility of exes, or perhaps you simply never thought it would happen to you. Regardless, now you had one. You had failed in a relationship, and there was someone out there who could attest to it.

Now that it had a taste of passion and love, the void in

you moaned and begged to be replaced and filled, more than ever.

You didn't know what to do. You floundered and flopped around, a fish on a boat hoping to go somewhere, anywhere. There were nights when you longed for him so much you stayed up for hours, freezing in your icebox bedroom, writing letters to him that he would never read. You missed him, but you were starved for a companion—a soul.

You returned to the Internet. While older men resumed their message-sending, you sent off your own to those you found different. Few replied, and fewer still seemed interested. Once again, there wasn't anyone like you. Maybe there never would be again. And from that doubt, I was conceived.

The dam began to crack. Water trickled through. The more you searched, the more conversations you had, and the more frustrated you became.

I remember that night. You started to die, and I was born.

As usual, you were online, not looking for anything specific, yet searching for relief from the aching aftershocks. You remembered thinking repeatedly, as if it were a mantra, that *someone* had to be out there for you.

That day, something stirred inside you. Your head was foggy; the compass needle was spinning round and round, so that when he—thirty-eight, twice your age—sent you an instant message, instead of turning him away on impulse, you gave him words.

There I was: slithering out of you, twisted together from the ugly words and images you learned from men, like Frankenstein's monster. Initially, you weren't sure what to make of me; you cautiously approached me as I mumbled lines and giggled when you actually typed and sent them. With every syllable, I grew stronger. These words led to darkness, and you knew it. But still you pressed on, half excited by where the trail would lead, half stoned on grief. When he informed you that he lived down on Main Street, less than a half-hour bus ride away, I screeched into your ear to go. We fought and wrestled for what seemed like hours, but I had an advantage: I knew all your moves. Pinned down, you picked up your wallet, keys, and cellphone, and hurried out before you realized you would regret it.

Next to his front door, there was a string of buoys, like the small ones that float in public pools, dividing lanes. The little gourds were sun-bleached, colours faded to pale hues—dried blood red, the green a dying grass. You loitered in the front for a bit, unsure of how this whole thing worked until he texted you to come on up through the back, and up the stairs. The sundeck was like your house, high and sheltered.

He opened the door for you when you got there, and you were surprised at his shortness. There was a friendly smile on his face, and he told you to come in. You took off your shoes, and tried to make conversation, as if he were a friend. There was a smell in his house that you couldn't quite place; sour, yet musky. The smell of a strange house with Axe or something still lingering in the air. You weren't sure if you liked it or not. He told you that his roommate was out for a few hours, and led you like a boatman silently down the carpeted hall to his bedroom.

Family Guy was on the television. You commented that

you didn't like *Family Guy* in an attempt to delay the inevitable. He patted the spot next to him on the bed and flipped the channel to a re-run of *South Park*. You lay down, heart beating out of control. The show wasn't particularly interesting or funny, but you stared at the TV fixatedly while out of the corner of your eye, he shuffled closer and closer. You continued watching as he put his hand on you, rubbing your body through your t-shirt.

That was when I grabbed you and shoved you into a cage, slamming shut the metal gate.

Now in control, I stared at the screen as he glanced at me, then touched me everywhere. You could feel it too, and every touch made you scream louder and louder.

It's not right! It's not right! Stop it!

The words echoed, the sound of iron clanging throughout every part of me. But I ignored it all. You shrieked from the prison as he removed my clothes, howled as he fondled me. My eyes glazed over, indifferent, as he looked up before he swallowed me. I felt nothing. It was nothing.

When he knelt in front of me, exposing his ass, I could hear you sobbing. Every time I thrust, my legs wobbled as if I was learning how to stand, and I wondered how he would react if I collapsed. I closed my eyes and thought of my ex, and hoped it was enough to keep me hard and get through it.

Like all things, it ended. I opened the cage, handing you back the reins, and saw your crumpled body, tears up to your knees. You sat in the corner and stared past me, at nothing. After a while, you crawled out, mumbling to yourself, "How could you? Never again, never again..." Wishful thinking, but the box was now wide open.

Outside, you dragged your feet on the cold sidewalk in a daze. There was something in your gut, churning, and you could never name it until now.

Me, kicking inside like a fetus, waiting to come out and play.

With every body, you grew weaker and weaker, bruised more and more every time I pushed you back into the cage: the tall man, the short friend, the withered model, and other names and faces you've buried with dirty hands. I exchanged more bodily fluids than words. There were times when you gagged on a stranger's stench and nearly vomited after. The more I abused this body, the less we both felt.

Eventually, when the moment came, you were a trained animal, walking yourself to the cage door. Routine. And after, when I opened the door, you no longer moved from the corner or glared at me. There were no more words. You simply sat there, impersonating a statue, staring at nothing.

I didn't notice when it happened, but one day, you were simply gone. When I searched for you, I found you unconscious, on life support. In fact, the real joke was on me: we shared the same blood. Traces of your ideas flickered in my mind each time I stained our body. True, I no longer had to bother with the cage, but whenever I saw you, I remembered what I used to be. I shook you and cried for you, but you lay there, silently condemning me.

I won. But there wasn't anything to celebrate.

Whoever said that we get wiser with age didn't know me. I became one of those lost souls I never imagined I would be, wandering aimlessly onto the next easy act.

Nevertheless, when men lure me with familiar siren-like words, I've begun to hear your voice whispering in my ear. When I look at you, damaged but bandaged, I swear I see the faintest twitch. I feel your hand guiding mine as I type:

Sorry, I'm busy tonight.

COLD WAR

I was made to believe there's something wrong with me
and it hurts my heart,
Lord have mercy, ain't it plain to see?
– "Cold War" by Janelle Monáe

THE draft coming from the bay window above me in my bedroom leaks cold winter air across the fine hairs on my arm. I hunch over the laptop on my desk, the nearby lamp showering light across the screen: blue unclicked links against the '90s-looking, white background scheme of the Craigslist "men seeking men" page. Not knowing where to start, I filter the ads by age and try my best to not be too grossed- and creeped out by the vulgar language and the explicit photos that I wonder how people are able to share publicly: "Daddy looking for son," "In serious need of cum" [sic], and the straightforward "come over and fuck my smooth ass" are titles that I want to assume are slightly off-putting to other nineteen-year-old gay guys and not only me. Despite being on the romance/long-term-relationship page, it seems clear that those using Craigslist are not looking for the same kind of relationship I am. I know I should probably stop, but I am propelled by hope that amongst the badly written sex ads, there stands someone waving his hand in the air. Someone like me, someone I could fall in love with.

After some perusing, I come across an ad that, at first, seems to be semi-grammatically correct and understandable: he is twenty-one, looking for dates and friends, and has posted a few pictures of himself shirtless (and not bending over). On the scale of crazy/creepy to sane, he seems to be relatively mentally sound. Perhaps my persistence through the trauma of seeing close-ups of unshaved anuses has finally paid off.

Suddenly, something makes me stop reading. I find myself staring at the screen for a few seconds, almost expecting the words and letters to re-arrange themselves into another phrase because I swear I must have misread. It takes me a few moments to realize that the words are there and they are not going away.

No Asians. Sorry it's just a preference.

My thought process is derailed for about a minute as I gape, astounded. All I can muster is a question.

How... why would someone say that?

It is a question that, upon seeing it everywhere in the years to come, I gradually stop asking.

***

Answering the question I had when I was nineteen isn't easy. Sexual racism is a complex subject that involves issues such as the fragmentation of the gay community, the differences between preferences and requirements, the social conditioning of attraction through things like media, culture, and porn, and the acceptance and passivity of this kind of language. Sound like too much? It's so complicated, it's no wonder gay guys would rather not think about unraveling this mess.

At first, I think no one is interested in having an honest discussion about an intellectual, semi-controversial topic that points the finger back at ourselves and our community. I remember when, a few months after my initiation on Craigslist, I stumbled across another ad that took me by surprise—in a different way.

"There is more than one kind of Asian. We don't all come from China," the anonymous poster declared. "Stop saying mean things about Asians."

Wow, I thought. All this sexual-racism stuff seemed so everyday, so casual, so accepted by everyone. And here was someone who was bluntly pointing it out. *Yes! Someone finally said it! People are going to change now.*

As I scrolled up the page to newer ads, there was a reply: "Take your ideas elsewhere. Let's keep Craigslist the way it is by letting guys hook up with guys."

And that was that. No more rebuttals, no more discussion. Return to homeostasis. Return to finding dicks and mouths and ass and excluding entire ethnic groups.

More recently, while using Jack'd, an app similar to Grindr except less sketchy and less, well, Grindr-y, I found a profile from an Asian guy who wrote "not into sticky rice" on his profile. Since this sounded vaguely racist, and as someone who was unaccustomed to a lot of today's slang, I had to look this one up.

"A homosexual Asian male who is sexually attracted exclusively to other homosexual Asian males," Urban Dictionary informed me. Well, that wasn't nice, to say the least. Yet the phrasing of "not into sticky rice" was unclear to me, and I found myself curious about what he meant. So naturally I had to inquire. First, I introduced myself—through my love of Chinese cuisine, nonetheless.

"What's wrong with sticky rice? It's great!" I sent. A response came a few minutes later.

"I'm racist. Deal with it."

Well, obvious self-declared racism aside, the part-time Writing Tutor in me was still wondering about the clarity of that sentence. "Are you saying you don't like Asians who like other Asian guys or are you saying you don't like other Asian guys?" Send.

I didn't get an answer a few minutes later like before; instead, he blocked me. It seemed no one wanted to talk about this, or at least, it didn't make for very titillating conversation. How can we address a problem, let alone find a solution, if no one is willing to bring it up?

So, when I ask my gay friends for their thoughts, I expect them to be equally uncomfortable and resistant to the topic. Surprisingly, they open up easily and have lots to say—just not what I expect.

"I'm sorry but you can't make sexual preference a racist thing."

"I think it's okay, and I don't think it's racism. It's a preference."

"For some reason, something about dating and sex and relationships changes how I feel about it. I just don't know why."

"Grindr is not about race. It is more about attraction. If someone finds me unattractive, I am okay with that."

My friends—and others, no doubt—don't seem to think it's racist to say things like "No Asians" or "No Indians" or even worse, jaw-droppingly awful phrases such as "No rice" and "No chocolate." Of the guys who said the four quotes above, two are Asian, one is Indian, and one is white. Minorities are the most targeted groups of sexual racism, and yet my friends don't believe it is racist behaviour or language. I thought for sure they would have had the same experiences as me, that they would feel similarly outraged, excluded, and defeated by members of our own community.

Maybe I need to back up a second before continuing with this. Is this type of talk even racist language? Is there racism in the gay community at all? Numerous academic studies confirm it.[1234] To me, the answer is obvious: no shit. From the very beginning, this kind of language has always struck me as extremely and obviously discriminatory, not to mention offensive.

By the end of the night, after texting a whole bunch of my friends who not only seem okay with coming across phrases that openly exclude them but argue that it is not racist language, I feel like a crazy person, like I've been gaslighted.

[1] Denton Callander, Martin Holt, and Christy E. Newman, "'Not Everyone's Gonna Like Me': Accounting for Race and Racism in Sex and Dating Web Services for Gay and Bisexual Men," *Ethnicities* 16, no. 1 (February 2016): 3–21. https://doi.org/10.1177/1468796815581428.

[2] Derek Ruez, "'I Never Felt Targeted as an Asian...until I Went to a Gay Pub': Sexual Racism and the Aesthetic Geographies of the Bad Encounter," *Environment and Planning A: Economy and Space* 49, no. 4 (April 2017): 893–910. https://doi.org/10.1177/0308518X16680817.

[3] Tony Ayres, "China Doll – The Experience of Being a Gay Chinese Australian," *Journal of Homosexuality* 36, 3–4 (August 1999): 87–97. https://doi.org/10.1300/J082v36n03_05

[4] Gilbert Caluya, "The (Gay) Scene of Racism: Face, Shame and Gay Asian Males," *Acrawsa* vol. 2 no. 2, (2006).

Like I am a scientist researching climate change and everyone laughs at me when the data clearly show a trend in rising global temperatures.

"But it's so obvious! It's right there!" I say, pointing exasperatedly at graphs and charts that are filled with alarming red lines while everyone exits the room, muttering to each other, "It's a natural cycle, dimwit."

Is a problem valid if people don't view it as a problem, or if only a minority considers it as a problem?

***

'Not into black; Asian; etc.'...

Translation: No matter how attractive you may be, you are inherently ugly due entirely to your race.

– Comment on douchebagsofgrindr.com

"I really don't see what's wrong with people having sexual preferences."

Oh, if I had a penny every time I came across that phrase, I could buy a million-dollar house in the ridiculously expensive housing market that is Vancouver.

Perhaps one of the reasons gay men justify their language is through the argument that it is simply a "preference," and that everyone has them. If everyone has preferences, and they are simply voicing how some exclude certain races, then theoretically, no one should feel bad, right? I have seen countless people online telling others to "get over it." No hard feelings, no harm done. Keep calm, shut the fuck up, and carry on.

Except that the word "preference" denotes choice and consideration. If I say that I prefer vanilla to chocolate ice cream, it means that if there was one bowl of vanilla and one bowl of chocolate on a table and I could only choose one, I would go with vanilla. But if there was only chocolate sitting all by its lonesome, I would happily devour it too. When men specify, "No Asians, sorry just a preference," that is not a preference. What they really mean is, "Sorry, just a requirement." If I were the only one in the room (the city, the continent, the world), their answer would still be no (or at least that is what is implied by their statement). I will never be considered. And not just me; the entire ethnically diverse umbrella of people considered "Asian" is automatically ignored, as if there never has and never will be anyone they find attractive from the continent that boasts 60% of the world's population. But "It's just a requirement" doesn't quite have the same ring or innocence to it as "preference." God forbid they should come off as the racists that they are.

In the months following my Craigslist introduction, I branch out to other sites as well: Gay.com and Manhunt, among others. When I begin online dating, I send out numerous messages and emails to people, trying to be witty and clever and charming, to win their hearts and minds. But despite the myriad of attempts, I mostly receive one response: silence.

Am I saying too many things? Am I being weird? Are my pictures not naked enough? Are my messages even getting through? I find myself asking time and time again. I am left to assume by their silence that they are not interested, but why not? I never know because no one tells me. And then, when someone bluntly replies, "I'm not into Asians," it is all I have to latch onto. Over the next few years, every time someone fails to respond, which is more than I keep track of, instead of any other possibilities for their rejection, a little buzzer goes off in my mind, telling me there is only one reason. The colour of my skin.

Perhaps what people do not realize is how racism feels, how it weasels its way deep into your skin and crawls up your brain, infecting it and the way you see the world. There is little empathy, so there is little change in society. And I am tired, so tired of it all, of everyone's complacency.

At the start of the AIDS epidemic in the '80s, writer Larry Kramer was angry. He got a lot done with that anger, confronting both the gay community and society at large for their lack of action and concern. Originally, I set out to write an essay to try and illuminate this issue of sexual racism, but my friends tell themselves they do not experience it, and I did not want to make this all about myself.

But I am pissed off.

***

Slanty eye, no reply
   – A profile on Grindr

In her revealing and fascinating PhD dissertation with the University of Washington titled "Sexual Racism in Gay Communities: Negotiating the Ethnosexual Marketplace," Mary

Dianne Plummer studies sexual racism in Seattle's gay community.[5] She discovers a hierarchy of desired races in the gay community, with whites at the top and Asians at the bottom; all participants in the study confirm this pecking order. In Vancouver, it is much the same: "No fats, femmes, and Asians," the personal ads constantly say, immediately ranking me on the lowest level of desirability.

I send messages to white guys, Asian guys, Middle Eastern guys, mixed guys, all of whom come across to me as interesting—personality-wise, that is—in some way. *Don't be afraid to say hi!* some of them exclaim on their profiles or ads. And when I do, most times they do not. I examine myself in the mirror more often, wishing I could unzip my hairless skin and climb into a paler suit with lighter hair and eyes and a beard, one with muscles and meat instead of my genetically scrawny frame. As much as I loathe the term, maybe I am just a "banana" whose peel repels everyone. I know I can be a good boyfriend; I have known it since I was a teenager. And yet no one seems to care because of the barrier that is my skin. When my friends tell me that these kinds of guys are not worth my time, I cannot help but feel the opposite—I am not worthy of their time.

One day, after coming across profiles that tell me I am unwanted, and weary of being ignored over and over again on Manhunt, a hookup site, I decide to do an experiment: I create a new profile and fill out almost all the info except ethnicity, which I leave blank. I skip uploading a photo and jump right into the site and begin messaging guys around me

[5] Mary Dianne Plummer, "Sexual Racism in Gay Communities: Negotiating the Ethnosexual Marketplace," (PhD diss., University of Washington, 2007).

(while also dumbing down my language a little).

Within minutes, the screen flashes at me: new messages. I talk with one guy who also does not have a photo and after chatting with him a bit, I disclose my experiment to him. He says he can relate, that it can be harsh and unfair in the gay hookup world. Others, who respond to me at first, stop messaging coincidentally after I send them my real picture. It seems clear to me what the reason is. After the experiment is over, the sad realization hits me.

I am more desirable being ambiguous/anonymous than I am being myself.

***

I put a picture up [on Craigslist] and maybe a day later I'll get 10 replies from older white men telling me 'Yeah, I love smooth little Asian boys.'

– Participant from Plummer's dissertation

"Overt race-based sexual rejection coupled with racial fetishization can serve to persuade the individual of the legitimacy of their low self-worth," Plummer notes.

To be fair, I do get some messages, many of which are from older (usually late thirties and over) white men who seem to find me desirable simply for being young and Asian. It is flattering at first, but quickly becomes tiresome and frustrating that, in combination with not receiving messages from those I attempt to contact, the only thing I seem to get is white men who constantly want to know "Where are you from?" (Me:

"Vancouver") followed by "No, where are you really from?" They tell me they want me to come over and spend time with them. "We can just hang out, take it slow," they coo, and upon encountering words like these endlessly on repeat, I ultimately stop believing it. And I don't even have to receive messages; "Looking to date an Asian guy," "seeking smooth Asian" from 40+ white men make it clear to me who wants my body and who I should want. There are rarely any ads or profiles from other young guys who specifically look for Asian guys.

I start to catch on that it might be because I am not being clear enough in my profiles, but even when I insert that I am looking for men around my age, I continue to receive these messages, as if by being both gay and Asian, I must, by default, be effeminate, a bottom, and into older white men (I am not a bottom and don't consider myself to be particularly feminine, although gender expression is a whole other topic).

I have never had an interest in dating someone old enough to be a "daddy." Maybe I will in the future, who knows, but not now. Message after message, site after site, stare after stare, it is the same. In the eyes of not only white men but probably all gay men who stereotype, being Canadian is irrelevant; I am a shiny, exotic object, ready and willing for a white saviour to take my smooth body. It is almost enough to make me give up on dating and looking for someone altogether.

Is this all I can get, all I deserve? Surely, it can't be. But maybe it is… maybe this is my fate. Maybe I should try looking at older guys differently. Or just get used to it, I think time and time again.

***

I'd find all these hot guys that I wanted to hook up with. They rejected me. They were saying, 'Oh, I'm not into Asians. You're not my type.' So it kind of led me to believe I was - I was horrible for my self-esteem.

– Participant in Plummer's study

Sexual racism, according to Plummer's findings, may result in "lower personal self-esteem and impaired psychological functioning" for those unlucky enough to experience it.

When I peruse Craigslist, Grindr, or Jack'd, usually just for kicks, I skim for keywords identifying race: "no Asians," "not into Asians," and other variations. Upon reading these phrases, I try to overlook the hurt gently punching me in the stomach. Similarly, for profiles that say "whites are a plus" but do not state anything about Asians, my gut tells me to move on. *What they probably mean is they're only into white guys, so don't even try,* the voice in my head translates. For profiles that do not mention race whatsoever, I tell myself guys wouldn't be interested in me anyway. *Why spend my time saying hi when I know all I'm going to get is more rejection? No, it's smarter not to try at all.*

This mentality extends itself to more than just the virtual world. When I stroll down Davie Street or through the West End, I see pairs of attractive white men together. Meanwhile, everyone seems to look through me as I attempt to make eye contact. When guys compliment me on my looks, such as my friend John who called me "pretty," my reflex response is, "Liar." Even when they insist, I do not believe it or feel it. It wasn't like I didn't have evidence to back up my beliefs; I had been rejected for years because for one reason or another, I was not attractive in all their eyes.

It's not as if media and pop culture don't reinforce this in some way. From *Queer as Folk* to *The New Normal* to *Glee,* to gay celebrities like Neil Patrick Harris and David Burtka, to ripped guys in porn, white guys get together with other white guys. It might as well be a fact. Minorities just kind of... aren't there. Whenever I come across a good-looking, interesting white guy around my age, I can't help but think he is looking for another white dude who has big pecs and a six-pack, a car, and a well-paying, secure job (i.e., not a writer).

With my second boyfriend G., who was Latino, I felt the need to tell him that I was insecure about being in a relationship, and I questioned, multiple times, why he was with someone as unattractive and undesirable as myself. On multiple instances he assured me, but it wasn't enough. I serenaded him with a song called "Good Enough"; I pretended to be cool with it when he and a straight male friend flirted with each other in front of me for fun. Once, I held off on texting him to see how long it would take for him to text me. Three days later, he finally said hi, which I interpreted as him not needing me in his life. When he went to a club with some friends, I imagined him getting hit on by other, more attractive men, muscled men with body hair like the models in the porn stash on his computer. Then he would wonder why he was with me when he was so wanted, so desired by better-looking guys, and that would be the end of me. Traded in for something better.

***

Placing gay Asian men in a larger societal framework, we see that
they are devalued within their ethnic community due to their sex-
ual orientation, devalued within the gay community due to their
race, and furthermore, marginalized and oppressed in the larger
American culture due to both aspects of their identity.

   – From Plummer's dissertation

Is the onus on victims of racism to not feel like victims—to, in a way, "get over it," as they say?

I don't think I can do this. I know—I feel—the power of words too much to simply devalue them, even if the words are from strangers or jerks. I cannot help but feel my pulse rise, my neck flush with heat and rage whenever I read, "No Asians, sorry it's just a preference." Apology not accepted.

Plummer describes how gay men of colour combat sexual racism by forming social supports and groups. A site like douchebagsofgrindr.com provides a virtual kind of social support group where people can vent and rant about issues that are plaguing the gay community.

Lucas and I first messaged each other on a dating site, and when we met in person, we bonded over stories of racist jerks; it felt strangely freeing, almost therapeutic, to talk to someone who shared the same beliefs at long last.

"I feel so much less crazy," I confided to him with relief.

But is talking amongst fellow sufferers really the best we can do? I imagine something akin to men huddled around a fire, showing their scars and wounds to one another. They whimper from recalling their painful journeys in a harsh, bitter world. But when the fire dies, they must venture out and brave the world once more.

A greater change would be preventing sexual racism altogether and educating others. In that case, maybe it is the world that should change, not the victims. Another website, the now defunct endracismandhomophobia.tumblr.com, is a helpful one. On the site, "Gay School 101" attempts to explain and educate gay men about the many problems we have internalized or normalized, like hypermasculinity, femmephobia, and this "straight-acting" thing that many gay men vehemently believe in. It's a great educational tool, I must admit, but I don't think this is a site that ever got a million hits; this especially since there are those out there, like my friends, who, even after discussion and debate, still believe it is simply an everyday part of life. Or as one commenter on Douchebags of Grindr says about a featured Grindr user being racist, "You see this all the time on Grindr. This isn't even that douchey." It seems like sexual racism is now a systemic problem that has been so normalized, many can't even begin seeing it as an issue.

One night, I invited a young Asian guy over to my place. When he arrived, I regretted it. He was young, a little immature, and I didn't want to hook up, just felt a little lonely. The two of us sat on my bed, chatting, with me fending off his advances (I was glad he was not offended that I didn't want to have sex). Somehow, we got on the topic of school, and I told him about racism in the gay community. Like my friends, he didn't think it was an issue. I wanted to kick him out.

But I saw this as a chance to be patient, to educate. When I brought in Plummer's research about the depression, low

self-esteem and self-worth, and self-sabotaging of relationships of those who experienced sexual racism, he listened. We
discussed. By the end, he threw his hands up in the air. "That
sounds awful! Why don't we do something about it?" He
paused for a moment. "We can make posters with facts about
how this hurts people and post them downtown, along Davie
Street!" he suggested, suddenly excited. "We can be the start."

After passionately arguing my case, I sighed. "I don't know.
I don't know if it will really do anything, and I don't know if
anyone will care. If they don't give a shit online, why would
they give a shit in the real world?"

Our inspiration for revolution died that night after he left.

I want to think we can remedy this; I want to be hopeful. Gay men have proven throughout history that we can be
activists against society and oppressors. However, I am skep-
tical whether or not we can reform ourselves. I like to think
sharing our stories about how racism has affected us, instead
of keeping everything to ourselves and internalizing our pain,
will spark discussion and change, but who knows if that will
be sufficient.

For the few days during which I have been writing this
personal essay, I've had a tab open on my Internet browser of
a profile on Plenty of Fish. The guy in the profile is twenty-six,
handsome, and white. In his lengthy blurb about who he is,
he mentions being attracted to "sapiophiles." I have to look
this word up too; Urban Dictionary defines a sapiophile as a
person sexually attracted to intelligent people. I like this a lot.

When I scroll through his pictures, I imagine him posing with someone who is a few years older, has a buzz cut,

probably works in business, and does the Grouse Grind on the weekends. Imaginary Soulmate, whose name is Jason or Vince, is a little short, about 5'7", but he's masculine, has a solid build and a nice smile. This guy may not be very opinionated about social-political issues, but it doesn't really matter because he's good in bed and he makes an adequate boyfriend and they'll both live happily ever after.

Further down on his profile, in a short paragraph about what he is looking for, Handsome Guy mentions, "if muscles, bone structure, a lack of effeminacy and preferred sexual position are your 4 big compatibility indicators, with social/professional status and a mutual proclivity for travel and the outdoors rounding out numbers 5 and 6 (when neither party has likely done much more than visit a Mexican all-inclusive and saunter up the Grouse Grind once or twice), messaging me is probably a waste of both our time."

My fantasy of the two of them together crumbles as I read this. I don't know what to think now, except *Is it bad to think someone is wonderful based on one very long sentence?*

There is nothing about race on his profile. The two sides of me—one telling me it is a waste of time because of my race, and the other saying I will never know because this guy is clearly intellectual and self-aware of the troubles plaguing society—have been debating for days. *What if he's just like everyone else? What if he's not?*

I take a breath and place my fingers on the keyboard.

"Yello, from one sapiophile to another. How goes life?"

And for a moment, I believe this could be the start of something special, that perhaps I have found the exception to the rule. The one who could change my mind and give me hope. We will be an example to our friends that race does not matter. He will share my stories of woe with his friends, who will turn a new leaf and eventually call out those who use racist language. When guys hit on him, he will point out my lanky Chinese body in the crowd and confidently inform them, "He's my boyfriend" to their confused and stunned faces. Yes, we will be radical partners in crime, changing society one mind at a time for many, many years. And it will have all begun with one simple message on an online dating site.

I don't receive a reply.

ALL THE WAYS TO SAY I'M GAY

At seven years old, in the third grade

LIKE all the other primaries (kindergarteners to third graders), we were sprinting and chasing each other like feral animals during recess and lunch. In those days (and likely still today), there were always insults at any moment, even if we didn't know what they truly meant. Someone mentioned these words, one by one, and like other taboo, grownup words, we whispered them with cupped hands into beckoning ears, spreading them like germs.

But on this particular day, it was a special word.

"GAY!"

Everyone was shouting it—and all its variations—at each other like rocks flung from slingshots, hoping to bruise: "You're gay!" "You're gayer!" "You're soooooo gay, you're the gayest!" Even at seven years old, I knew I liked other boys, but I never knew there existed any sort of word for it. So, when I asked a classmate what this "gay" thing meant, she told me it was when boys like other boys, and girls like other girls. It also meant happy, but that wasn't nearly as fun as the other meaning.

I finally found the word that I could use to describe myself. And it was such a nice word too: it rhymed with "Yay!", also quite an enjoyable thing to say.

While the other kids squealed and screamed to whatever game they were playing, I skipped around the woodchip-softened playground on my own, gleefully announcing, "I'm gay! I'm gay!" to no one/everyone/mostly myself. Nobody seemed to care (or hear me); no one laughed or stared or beat me up.

I was so elated and excited to express my newfound revelation to everyone that when I spied the adult supervisor sitting on one of the pale blue benches, I had to tell her too. I snuck up behind her as quietly as a giddy kid possibly could, then leaned in and said in her ear, "I'm gay"—quite gaily, I might add.

Before she could do anything, I frolicked away, amazed at my own boldness; unfortunately, I heard her calling to me from behind, commanding me to stop and come back. I attempted to avoid confrontation with her by talking with my friend Jessica, who conveniently happened to be nearby, but the supervisor didn't let up. She approached me, and being the adult-fearing youngster I was, I gave her my attention.

"Where did you hear that word?" she asked, her face stone-serious. "The only meaning for that word is happy. It doesn't mean anything else. Don't you ever think it means anything else. Do you understand?"

As she lectured me, I began to cry. By the time she asked that final question, all I could do was manage a slight nod. She dismissed me, and I ran off to the bathroom a blubbering mess, wondering why and how this strange lady thought she knew me better than I knew myself.

It would be another ten years before I was physically able to say the word again.

***

At fourteen years old, to my diary

The idea terrified me for days.

I didn't want anyone to know, but at the same time, I wanted—no, needed—someone to know. So, after mulling over it, when the slits of light underneath the doors of my mom and sister's rooms flicked off to darkness, I locked my bedroom door and knelt in front of the big drawer on the left side of my desk. Sticking nearly my entire arm in, I groped around used binders and my clarinet gear before finding the journal I had stashed months ago.

I opened it to the next blank page and took a seat at the desk. With a black fine-tip pen in hand, I let out a slow, measured sigh as the trembling pen hovered above the page.

Not knowing where to begin, I started with small talk:

Jan. 6, 2003

Happy New Year! I went snowboarding at Whistler Blackcomb. It was so fun! Jessica got stuck in a ditch and we couldn't find her for about 15 minutes. To the important news now: the depression is really taking its toll. I'm so close to killing myself. Also, in stupid Cadets today, we had a "sports night" and by sports, we played Octopus Tag and other childish games. It was such a waste of time.

Okay, enough delay. Get to it. Now. I steadied my hand and gripped the pen harder.

> To add to my misery, my crush on Sean Dwyer has got
> me hallucinating what life would be like if he was my
> boyfriend. I'm so scared to tell anyone I'm

I couldn't. *It's just a word, an arrangement of letters,* I rationalized, but it wasn't enough because they weren't simply letters or strokes of black ink. That three-letter word was too big,
too powerful—I couldn't even say it aloud anymore. Besides
being a confession, it was a bomb, waiting to explode in the
eyes of whoever read this. I glanced at the locked door, then
around my room as if my ancestors, in their ancient silk robes
and peasant work clothes were hovering over my shoulder, invisible, waiting to see how the sentence would end. This bedroom could so easily not be my room anymore just by the act
of pressing this quivering pen to the lined paper of this book.

But for my sanity, I must.

> I'm so scared to tell anyone I'm gay because I keep
> thinking that they won't accept me for the way I am.
> And now, if for some weird reason I ask Sean if he can
> be my boyfriend, I'm so afraid he'll reject me. Then, he'll
> tell everyone that I'm gay and then I'll have no friends
> and everybody will think of me differently.

My hand lifted off the page for a second, letting the wild
thought of my mom snooping around my room and stum-
bling upon my notebook interrupt me.

If someone reads this, my life will be ruined.

***

At fourteen years old, to Aunt Wendy[6]

From: Aaron Chan
To: Aunt Wendy
Date: Sept. 6, 2003
Subject: The Secret Confessions of Aaron Chan

Dear Aunt Wendy,

How are you? I am okay, I guess, up till today. My mom is forcing me to go to Air Cadets for another year, starting this Monday. This sounds like I'm insane but I really need your help.

Last year, when I was in Cadets, I became very depressed and moody all the time. I tried to tell my mom I was going through depression but she didn't know what that was. I figured it was useless anyways, since I tried many times before and she still wouldn't change her mind. I started to think about taking my own life. I know this sounds crazy and that it's out of my character, but it is true. I really believed that it was the only way for me to get what I wanted, but of course there was something that stopped me. It wasn't school, grades, siblings, or anything out of the ordinary. I had a crush on

[6] When I was younger, I thought Aunt Wendy, who lived in Hawaii, was the cool relative in my family. She was the youngest aunt (whereas my mom was the eldest), spoke the best English, and was probably the most liberal/Westernized. I used to call her up and chat with her about school and life because I felt like she understood me miles better than my more conservative parents.

someone at my school. For the past year, they were the only thing holding me back from stupid decisions, like suicide. I wondered why I gave into things so easily. If I didn't have a crush, I might not be here today, though I am not quite sure.

When my mom first promised me and Maggie that we'd only spend a year at Cadets, I breathed a sigh of relief. I know she wants me to get a good job in the future, but she just sticks me in a course and expects me to like it. That is really mean.

This is my final plea. I don't know what else to do. I would like you to talk to my mom or something, to try and convince her to let me stop going to that terrible place. If she hears it from you, she just may change her mind. Tell her what I just told you, except for the crush part. I don't want her to know about that just yet, hehe. If you are still unconvinced that I am telling the truth, I can't say anything else. If you do not do anything, that's your decision. But you might wake up and find your "favorite" nephew is gone.

Love, Aaron

From: Aunt Wendy
To: Aaron Chan
Date: Sept. 7, 2003
Subject: Re: The Secret Confessions of Aaron Chan

Dear Aaron, my favorite nephew,

I am very concerned about your well-being and can only imagine the pain you must have suffered in the last few years. As soon as I finished reading your email, I telephoned your mommy and told her about your plea for help, except the crush you had on someone at school. At first, she was stubborn, as I explained to her your depression and thoughts about suicide, she began to listen.

Basically, she wants you and Maggie to learn something outside of school. She thinks that you and Maggie have a lot of idle time on hand, and are wasting precious time on the weekend by sleeping in late, etc. Are you willing to go learn another thing, say, Chinese school, or swimming, or Boy Scouts, to offset not having to go to Cadets?

As for the person you had a crush on, what happened?

I hope you will stay focused in school but feel free to email me if you need to talk to someone or have any questions about relationships or life. I will try my best to talk to you.

Take care.

Love,

Auntie Wendy

From: Aaron Chan
To: Aunt Wendy
Date: Sept. 7, 2003

I'm glad you phoned my mom. She negotiated with me after your phone call and I have to find another course outside of school to replace Cadets but if I don't, then I must go back there again. Right now, I am so relieved that I get to choose something else. As for my crush, I still like them but I just have one question: How do you know the difference between a crush and when you're in love?

Love, Aaron

From: Aunt Wendy
To: Aaron Chan
Date: Sept. 8, 2003

Dear Aaron,

I am glad your mom listened to your plea. As for the difference between having a crush and falling in love, there is a BIG difference.

Let me use myself as an example. When I was seventeen, I had a crush on my history teacher. I wondered where he lived, if he had a girlfriend, how many siblings he had, what kind of food he liked, etc. You name it, I wondered. I would sit up straight and listen to his teaching every class. When I saw him in the hallway, I would address him and hope he would remember me. My interest in him was, of course, not returned and not noticed. In a few months, my feelings for him went away, and I even wondered why I was interested in him in the first place. There were no broken hearts, no tears, and no sleepless nights, because the feeling was one-sided, silly, yet perfectly normal for a teenager. This is called a crush.

Aaron, it is perfectly normal to have a crush on someone you met. At first glance, that person may seem so nice and so perfect; however, it is more important to take the initiative to slowly get to know that person, and develop a friendship first.

Instead of putting that person on a pedestal, it is very important to get to know her and be her friend first. Most couples become friends first, lovers later.

Not until both parties enjoy each other's company so much that both agree to be exclusive with each other. When that occurs, you are in a relationship and in love. You cannot be in love with someone who is not even aware of your existence or feelings.

Even falling in love has a lot of heartaches, tears, and sleepless nights because a relationship requires a lot of patience, compromise, and sacrifice. More on that later, when you are in love.

Aaron, I know teenage years are very trying and confusing. I am here to do my best to help you through them. I hope I explained myself well.

By the way, why did you use the term "them" when referring to the people you have a crush on? Is there more than one person? Do they know you and have you talked to them?

Talk to you later.

Love,

Auntie Wendy

From: Aaron Chan
To: Aunt Wendy
Date: Sept. 8, 2003

Dear Aunt Wendy,

I understood your explanation of a crush and I thought

it was good, but it still didn't explain some of the things I felt. Your example has totally happened to me before but how can you tell if you're in love or if it's just a crush? There is only one person that I have a crush on, even though I used to like a few people. I used "them" because I think I have a crush on a guy, but I'm not sure.[7] It's really confusing for me right now, with my school life and all, and I might actually be gay. He was in some of my classes last year, and last week, I saw him smoking! And he's only fifteen!!! I have one class with him this year, but we're not really friends and we don't talk to each other. He knows me from last year though, because he was in my French class and he needed help sometimes. I would appreciate it if you wouldn't tell this to my mom, because I know she'll flip out and lecture me. My friends say those people are "traditional" and like everything the old-fashioned way. Anyhoo, I'm really happy about my life, now that I'm rid of all those bad things.

Love, Aaron

From: Aunt Wendy
To: Aaron Chan
Date: Sept. 8, 2003

Dear Aaron,

If the person doesn't even participate in a relationship with you, share the same feelings and emotions as you, it is

---

[7] I was sure. I lied because as liberal as she was, Aunt Wendy was still Chinese, straight, and from a different generation, so I believed she wouldn't/couldn't truly understand, that she would tell me it was a phase or that I couldn't know as I was only fourteen.

definitely a crush.

I wonder if you think you are gay because you are curious about what other guys do, compared to you, such as if they play a musical instrument, watch the same movies, like the same subjects, etc., or you are sexually attracted to them, such as, you want to touch and hold them? There is a difference between being curious about other males and being gay. Don't jump to conclusions too soon and label yourself as gay.[8]

If you are not sure whether you are gay at this point, don't think about it. Just concentrate on school, and in a few years, things will look clearer to you.

Also, are you attracted to girls in your school? Not all girls are like Florrie[9], Maggie, and your mom; there are some really decent, sweet, and intelligent girls out there. You will lose out if you don't get to know them. You should hang out with other girls and get to know the opposite sex.

Males and females are good complements of each other as they tend to think and feel differently. Don't close your doors to the opposite sex yet. It is premature to draw that conclusion.

Teenage years is one the most difficult stages in life because you know a lot more than being an adolescent, but yet you don't totally know who you are. In the process of finding who you are, you might become confused about things and people. Don't be afraid. Take your time to grow up and not label yourself so soon.

I am not going to tell your mom about our emails because I want to listen to what you feel and think, then share my

[8] I told you so.

[9] The nickname for my sister, Florence.

personal experiences with you, and hopefully provide some advice to you in the next few years.

Feel free to ask me any questions. I will be very honest with you.

Love,

Auntie Wendy

From: Aaron Chan

To: Aunt Wendy

Date: Sept. 9, 2003

Dear Aunt Wendy,

I understand about having a crush, but I really can't get him out of my head and when I saw him smoking, I really wanted to go over and yell at him for being so stupid. Every time I see his face, it makes me feel good, which sounds really weird... Also, he never really talked to me before until I helped him a bit in French class last year and then after that he talked to me a bit but this year, I only have one class with him and he has his own friends. I guess you could call him one of the stereotypical Caucasian guys that you would find in every high school that skateboard and stuff like that. I have friends that are girls but I don't really like any girl in particular at my school. I like them as friends but not in a love-way. What do you think my mom would say if I told her I liked guys?

Love, Aaron

From: Aunt Wendy

To: Aaron Chan
Date: Sept. 10, 2003

Dear Aaron,

Whatever you decide to do, tell or not tell your mom, DO NOT tell people in school that you might be gay. You might be bullied, verbally abused, or attacked by "traditionists." Be careful because gay people have been attacked and some even got killed in other cities. It might not be wise to come out of the closet now especially since you are still young and confused.

One more thing. The Caucasian you like now. Do you like him for his physical appearance or his athletic skills? Maybe it is admiration instead of attraction. Do you understand the difference between the two? Maybe you wish you had a big brother to protect and care about you, so you prefer being around males.

Anyway, don't jump to conclusions too soon and concentrate your energy on schoolwork.

Love,
Auntie Wendy

***

At fourteen, to my friends Chelsea and Ann

During the summer between the end of Grade 9 and the start of Grade 10, I made plans to hang out with my friends. Although school was out for the season, we decided to meet at our high school because we thought it was cool or something.

This is going to be the day, I thought as I got off the bus and walked across the lush green field to the two figures waiting down the hill for me. I had rehearsed the words in my head for days. Just two words. How hard could it be?

"Where's Lily?" I asked Ann and Chelsea. "And Joanne?"

Ann and Chelsea told me they couldn't make it.

I had hoped to come out to all four of them, but maybe starting with two was a better idea.

"I have something to tell you," I told my friends.

"Okay. What?"

As they waited for my revelation, I suddenly became too aware of the situation: I was going to tell them my secret that I had vowed I would never tell anybody. And what if they gossiped to everyone like it always happened in books? I could get bullied and no one would help me and I could have my face stuffed into a toilet in the boys' washroom and then I'd have to switch schools and oh my god what was I doing?

The words lodged in my throat, and I more or less stared back, slack-jawed.

"I... can't say it," was all I managed to utter.

"You can't do that!" they exclaimed. "If you don't tell us, we'll make you tell us!" Then they proceeded to chase me around the field, but as a former track-and-field athlete, I easily evaded capture. When we were all out of breath, we settled beneath the shade of a great maple tree just beyond the chain-link fence of the tennis courts of the school.

"So, what the hell is it?" Chelsea began the interrogation again.

Again, I faltered. But an idea came to me. "Guess."

Ann and Chelsea exchanged glances. "Do you like some-one?" Of course that was the first thing they asked.

I thought of Sean Dwyer, my biggest crush in the whole world and said yeah.

Now that that bridge had been crossed, I was sure the next part would be easy—but I had completely forgotten how heterosexist society is.

"Is it Megan Fu? Oh! Diane? What about Rachelle? Julia Stahl?"

"No, no, ew, and who?"

The more I denied their list of girls in our grade, the less they seemed to catch on. I had to give them a hint. "You're guessing the wrong *type* of people."

"So, what? You want us to name ugly people?" Ann retorted.

"No. Just think about it."

At this point, I was so terrified and embarrassed that they would get it that I put my red baseball cap on my face because I didn't want to see their expressions when they guessed right, and I didn't want them to see mine. After a pause, I heard one of them ask quietly, "Do you like men?"

Suddenly I felt like throwing up. "Yes," I choked. A brief moment of silence followed[10], and I braced myself for their reactions while gulping warm, moist air beneath the cap on my face.

"That's cool. I've always wanted a gay friend," Ann assured

[10] I learned two years later that during this time, Chelsea was apparently stuffing her mouth with bread to keep from laughing – not because the news was at all hilarious, but because it was so unexpected – and didn't want to seem insensitive to the disclo-sure of my secret. Or so she said.

me. "We should go shopping together!"

"Yeah, it doesn't change anything," Chelsea added. They promised I could trust them with my secret. Moments later, when my pulse returned to normal, I almost felt silly for believing my friends might have reacted badly.

"So, who do you like?"

"Guess."

Groans followed, then laughter.

"It's a good thing you told us and not Lily or Joanne," they mentioned after, as we walked together to the bus stop. "They're not as liberal as us."

***

At fourteen, to Lily

"Find out how compatible you are with your crush! Just click here to find out!" the hyperlink boasted in Lily's email. *This could be fun. Why not?* I thought.

The page directed me to type in my name, followed by the names of three people I wanted to check my compatibility with. I was really only curious about my chances with one person but I was required to put down two other names, so I typed in Chelsea and Lily for fun. In the third slot, I entered Sean Dwyer, my über-crush. I clicked the "See my results!" button and waited anxiously for the page to load.

I didn't know what to expect, but it definitely wasn't the page informing me, "The names of your crushes have been sent to the person who sent you the email! We hope you don't mind! ☺ ".

My eyes almost burst out of their sockets. "What the fuck? Fuck you, you fucking site!" I cursed at my computer. But my anger only lasted a moment, as I realized the true implications of the deception.

With lightning speed, I returned to my inbox and composed an email to Lily. "That email you just got from those evil people who calculate your percentage with your crush? Whatever you do, DON'T OPEN IT! PLEASE, LILY!"

When I hit the Send button, I let out the breath I didn't realize I had been holding. *What could be so bad about coming out to Lily?* It's not that I didn't want to come out to her, but more that she was a bit conservative, like some traditional Chinese people. I was unsure how she would react, and mostly feared she wouldn't understand. That and I had been completely unprepared to come out.

Later that day, I received a reply from Lily.

Aaron....

can i ask you something..you don't have to answer...and obviously it's none of my business... Again I am just being the nosy Lily..

YOU DON'T HAVE TO ANSWER...
but do you like the same gender?

You don't have to answer if you don't want to...
I won't pester you at school
but if you don't want to reply...write me an email and tell

me "It's none of my business!" okay?!

<('.')> LiLy <('.')>11

***

At fifteen, to my mom

Four days before my sixteenth birthday, I was sitting on my bed, cradling a guitar on my leg. An instructional book with extra-large pink musical notes for beginners was spread on the covers of the bed in front of me.

Knock, knock. Without waiting for an answer, my mom walked in and took a seat on the bed beside me. Wordless entries into my room meant the most serious of talks from my mother, and I braced myself for whatever was coming. I couldn't hold her gaze, and had to stare down at the book. Instead of the usual Cantonese she spoke to me with, she said, "I want you to tell me the truth," in measured, calm English, which she only reserved for the gravest discussions. "Are you gay?"

Yesterday, one of my sisters had caught me watching gay porn yet again on the computer. I assumed she told my mom. I had never thought about how I wanted to come out to my traditional Chinese mom, but I did not picture it happening

---

11 If you're wondering, nothing ever ended up happening between me and Sean Dwyer. I managed to have a few conversations with him during our time in high school. I believe the last time was when I was in my Wicca phase, and he had joked about how I should cast a "speed spell" on him so he could run faster during PE class. When I brought it up with him again later, he said he was joking, and that he was Roman Catholic and into Jesus, no doubt believing in the stereotypes of witchcraft. He also rejected my friend request on Facebook a few years later, so there's that too.

like this.

Like my coming out to Chelsea and Ann, saying yes was much easier than saying "I'm gay." So I said yes and continued to avert my eyes, now examining the polished wooden surface of the guitar. I could almost hear her mind churning, working up a response.

"You know this is not normal."

Having come across this argument plenty of times in the gay-themed YA novels I had been reading in the past year, I argued, almost like a script, that it was actually normal, that there were gay animals out there which proved homosexuality was natural. She countered, "Who wants their child to be gay?"

I recalled a quote from Alanis Morissette from an edition of *Xtra! West*. Morissette had mentioned that she would love to have a child who was gay, because she or he would be that much more special. I didn't think my immigrant Chinese mother would care what Alanis Morissette said or even knew who she was, so I held back on this. I answered with silence instead.

My mom drove her point further by pointing out that no one in our entire extended family was gay, so how could I be? I didn't have an answer to that (except that perhaps some of them weren't as straight as they seemed), and when I still didn't respond, she asked, "How come you didn't tell me?"

"You wouldn't be happy if you knew. I know you're homophobic." When I looked over at her, she gave me the stare I had come to recognize means she didn't understand the word or phrase I had said. "I know you don't like it," I simplified.

Her eyes looked sad, as if I disappointed her by not trusting and confiding in her, despite the arguments just now about how being gay wasn't normal.

"Well, why don't you try and change yourself?"

"I can't!"

"How do you know?"

"There's nothing to change!"

"Maybe you should go out with one of Maggie's friends." My sister's friends were also my friends—Chelsea, Ann, Lily. Obviously, they wouldn't want to go out with their (out) gay friend, not that I even wanted to date my friends.

"I don't want to go out with them, or any girl. Could you go out with a woman?"

For a change, I rendered my mother mute. Finally, as if aware of the feebleness of the excuse, she replied, "I don't have time to date."

She shook her head in confusion. "I still don't understand why you are gay. What made you this way?" Her face was full of concern, like I had confessed to having a terminal disease.

"Nothing made me this way," I said with a weary sigh. I was exhausted trying to explain myself when it seemed so clear. But my mom wouldn't let it go.

"Is it because of playing piano? You can stop lessons."

"What? No."

"Is it because of this Wicca thing you're into now?"[12]

"No! Mom, it's none of those things. It's just who I am."

Another pause, longer this time. I thought she finally un-

---

[12] For about two years, I was interested in Wicca and bought a beginner's Wicca kit. I didn't get that serious about it—mostly just simple incantations to feel good about myself, to have a good day, and to eventually find love. I was open about it with my family, but as hard as I tried to explain it to my mom, she never quite understood what it was or what I was doing.

derstood.

Then, "Do you want to go see a doctor?"

In the gay teen stories, both fiction and non-fiction, that I devoured voraciously and hid from my family, there were some unsympathetic, ignorant parents out there: they disowned their kids, verbally and physically abused them, sent them to conversion camp—even kicked them out of their homes. I knew that were I to come out to my parents, they would not take it well, but at least they would never believe the "gayness is a disease that needs treatment" misconception. I mean, my immigrant parents were conservative, but I believed—hoped, really—that having lived in Canada for decades would have influenced them to be more liberal themselves. I was sure they were not the idea of ultra-traditional families in China I pictured in my mind, ones who, to my limited knowledge of Chinese life due to never having lived in Asia before, forced their queer children to marry someone of the opposite sex to save face or simply rejected/disinherited them entirely. I guessed I was wrong.

"I'm not sick! There's nothing wrong with me." It was only then—when I looked up at my mother's knotted face, eyebrows like steeply slanting cliffs, with a mixture of concern and incomprehension—that I realized my mother didn't share this belief. She truly did believe there was something wrong with me. And if she thought I had some sort of disease, what else could she believe in? What else could she do to me?

There was something I needed to know. Trying to suppress the accumulating heaving in my abdomen, as if my diaphragm was punching upward at my throat, I managed to choke out between the increasing hiccupping sobs, "Do you still love me?"

She answered without hesitation. "Of course I love you. You are my son."

I had never heard her refer to me as her son. I couldn't hold back anymore, and I bawled. Tears fell between the strings of the guitar and the frets and dampened my shirt. I wrapped my arms around my mother and felt her squeeze me back. We both cried.

***

At fifteen, a mass email to classmates and friends (and one cousin)

It's funny how once you come out, you sometimes want to come out to everyone right away, right now.

Subject: Quiz on me (#2)
Date: Sat, 16 Jul 2005 23:49:51 -0700

Warning: it is actually very hard, but I think it shows who I am better.
Have fun trying to figure it out, if you've already read this much.

S Club13

PS. If you're wondering about a few of the questions

---

[13] I used to be a big fan of S Club and S Club 7 and I signed my name as such because I was oh so cool.

and my referring to boys, I will now just confirm your already long-term suspicions. I am gay! And proud! That just made everything a lot better...

***

At eighteen, to my father

"When are you gonna tell your dad?" Chelsea asked me every now and then. I was sure she was only teasing, but the reminders were enough. I did want to tell him, but I knew he was more traditional than my mom. He was the same man who randomly told me and my sisters in the car once that being gay wasn't natural. It also didn't help that my dad and I didn't have a very good relationship—or rather, we simply lacked one—since he hadn't been very present for the majority of his children's lives. On another occasion, he had told me how showing affection for one's kids wasn't how he was raised, and how his father was raised, and so on. It wasn't the Chinese way. And included in the Chinese way was hating on the gays.

After lunch with him one day, my dad parked the car down the street where I lived with my mom and sister. I opened with the classic line: "I have something to tell you," before he waited for me to say it.

"I'm gay."

It all happened easier than I thought, the word slipping out with some but relatively much less trouble. I hadn't really considered what he would specifically say or do, but I knew it likely was not going to be supportive.

"Do you have a boyfriend?"

It stunned me to hear him say that. I interpreted it as curiosity, a positive response. I told him I didn't.

"Well, I think you know that I already had a feeling. But you are what you are."

Maybe I was wrong about my parents; maybe my mom was actually the more traditional one. Maybe I had a Chinese dad who was cool with his gay son.

A couple of days later, Dad phoned the house. From my bedroom, I heard my mom speaking with him for a bit, and I continued with my homework before the obnoxious voices from the Chinese soap opera in the living room invaded my space. As I got up to turn down the TV's volume, my mom walked in. She handed me the phone with an expression I couldn't read.

"I have some things to say," Dad declared brusquely.

He started off telling me he had been thinking for the past two days about what I told him. "Being gay isn't right," he stated, and proceeded to list the many reasons why. Most of our conversation wasn't a conversation, but rather my dad going off and me bearing it because I was completely unprepared—that, and I had never argued with my father before.

Line after line, the barrage didn't stop:

"If you look at wild animals, it's always male and female. They look after their young. It's human nature."

"No one in the entire generation of Chans has ever been gay. So how can you be?"

"When you are gay, you have no desire to have a family, no

need to plan for the future, so you go out and party and have sex. Then you get diseases like AIDS. That's why young men die so early."

The one time I countered was when he claimed, "You can't have children. You can't pass down the family name."

"I can adopt," I said.

"Adoption isn't the Chinese way." I immediately recalled Aunt Wendy and her two recently adopted daughters, but didn't mention it.

"Don't tell anyone else that you are gay. Word goes around and people talk. Everyone knows each other."

After several minutes of one voice on the line, there was a pause. "I am disappointed in your choice," he said, concluding the call.

***

From eighteen-ish to twenty-three-ish, Chelsea introduces me to everyone:

It usually went something like this:

A nondescript function of some kind—anything from a birthday party to a fundraiser: Lights are dimmed, music plays. Perhaps there are some decorations and signs on the walls. The crowd is mostly YOUNG MEN and YOUNG WOMEN (twenties), dressed in casual clothing. There's a gentle murmur of voices permeating the air. Some hold alcoholic beverages in their hands as they converse with one another.

CHELSEA, friendly and casual, and AARON, introverted and awkward, enter. AARON scans the crowd and the space as CHELSEA spots FRIEND walking by.

FRIEND: Hey, Chelsea!

CHELSEA: Hey! How are you?

FRIEND: Good, good. You?

AARON subtly gives FRIEND the evil eye at the incorrect usage of grammar, who doesn't notice.

CHELSEA: I'm all right. We just got here.

FRIEND notices AARON standing awkwardly there.

FRIEND: Oh, and this is your—

AARON: No, I'm not—

CHELSEA: He's gay!

AARON glances over at CHELSEA as FRIEND looks slightly amused.

Everyone always thinks we're together, but we're not. And I have a boyfriend. Who isn't here.

AARON: Yeah… (*to FRIEND*) I'm Aaron.

FRIEND: I'm Friend. (*to CHELSEA*) Oh, there's Janet. I haven't seen her in, like, forever! I'm gonna go say hi. I'll see you in a bit, okay?

CHELSEA: Oh, I have to say hi to her later too. Okay, see you.

FRIEND exits.

(to *AARON*) Sorry I outed you. Again.

AARON: That's okay. You do it better than me anyway.

***

At twenty-one, to my cat, Batman

Chet Baker was crooning with his voice and trumpet in my living room. It was raining and chilly outside (as it usually was in Vancouver), but indoors, the heat of G.'s and my skin cycled through each other. Our hard-ons bumped against each other through our underwear as we awkwardly but joyously shuffled around in circles as Chet commanded us to get lost in each other's arms.

"Maoww!"

I looked down to see the familiar black-and-white fur of my cat, Batman[14], peering up at us. Batman had never seen me dance with anyone before, let alone another boy. I laughed, and we kept swaying as she repeatedly meowed and brushed up against us, like she was some sort of third-wheel partner. At first, I thought she probably wanted to join us, but perhaps it was more along the lines of, "What are you doing? Who is this and why is he pantless and why are you rubbing your crotches together? WHAT IS THIS?"

The following week, with my mom out of town for a few days, G. and I made plans to spend the night together. I ran a bubble bath, something I had never done before but had always thought would be romantic and fun. Within minutes, the bubbles dissipated and instead, we disappointingly soaked in what appeared to be regular warm water. It didn't help the romance that there wasn't much space in the tub for the two of us and was awkward to lie in, but oh well. We were both full of cheeky grins as I leaned over to kiss him and feel him up.

14 Named so because the black of her fur makes her appear like she has a Batman mask on. And don't get me started on why her name isn't Batwoman or Batgirl.

When I pulled away, I noticed something standing a few feet away outside of the bathroom. Since we were home alone, we had left the door open. And now, Batman stared at us, unblinking, her head tilted slightly to one side like a typical confused animal attempting to make sense of the sight.

"This is weird," G. noted. "We should've closed the door." We went back to our fun (but kept it PG-13 despite being naked in a tub) while she continued being a voyeur for a bit longer before disappearing. I realized later that if the slow dance wasn't enough of a hint that her owner was a giant, flaming gay, then being naked in water with another guy and sticking our tongues in each other's mouths should've done the trick.

Can animals even be homophobic? I wondered. *What if she doesn't come and sleep with me at the foot of my bed like she does every night? What if she would rather be with a straight owner?*

That night, when G. and I went to bed, there was no sight of Batman. I figured she was not comfortable with G. around since he was still somewhat new to her, but I couldn't help thinking she might not have liked this other side of me.

The following morning, I asked G. if he ever felt or saw Batman come and sleep with us.

"At one point, she jumped up on the bed," he recalled. So she still liked me after all. I sighed a little with relief.

He continued, "But I didn't know what it was, so I kicked it and she jumped off."

Maybe her approval of my boyfriend will take a bit more work.

***

In my twenties, coming out to the world

One of the following:

1.

"What's your memoir about?"

"Oh, about growing up in a conservative Chinese family in Vancouver, juggling those two often conflicting identities, and... uh, yeah."

There's also a third identity in there, and even though my mind tells me to just say the damn word, I can't. I've been out (arguably) since I was seven and here I am, now twenty-five, and I can't tell a curious stranger—who, as a hippie-looking, likely super-liberal East Van woman—surely wouldn't have cared the slightest (in fact, she probably would've thought it was interesting). And yet, not a week prior, I had written a book proposal for a creative writing class about my memoir, confidently touting the unabashed gayness of it as a unique perspective and selling point.

"Well, that sounds pretty interesting," the hippie chick says.

I smile and nod, believing no doubt that she is unimpressed and only saying that to be polite. I'm left to wonder if I'll be able to properly pitch my memoir when it gets published.

2.

"So, how's your love life?" I'll ask someone once I feel comfortable enough with him/her/them. It's my go-to, semi-joking phrase. They usually laugh, give a short answer ("Good" or "Non-existent"), and as expected, point the question back at me.

"Oh, my love life is fine. But back to you, how did you two meet?" I'll say. Most of the time, people see through the deflection ruse and only when they press on do I relinquish more details.

"We met online... It's been a couple years now... *He* graduated in kinesiology." Then I brace for their reply, my eyes locked onto their faces for any signs of a negative reaction: a grimace, a tight pursing of the lips, the furrowing of the eyebrows. But there is never any of that. It is always met with neutrality.

"Oh, kinesiology, that's interesting. Did you get to see each other a lot while you were in school?"

I'm left to wonder why I ever built things up in the first place.

3.

"Let's start with Aaron's piece, 'The Birth and Death of You and Me.' What did you enjoy about it?" the instructor addresses the class sitting cramped in a circle around wooden tables.

There's a brief moment of silence, which my mind translates as, *Nothing. Everyone hated it and it doesn't even work as a memoir piece. You totally blew someone to get into the program, right? Because there's clearly no other way you should be here.*

Kathleen starts. "As a straight woman, I found it really relatable, even though the piece is about the narrator's awful sexual experience."

I exhale audibly, and some glance my way. My classmates discuss the piece like every other piece in our creative nonfiction workshop class at UBC. I figured I had to come out to them at some point if I'm going to be writing about myself, so why not get it over with?

I'm not sure I even came out in person to any of my classmates during my time at university; the overwhelming majority of the material I wrote was so gay—in every genre, not only nonfiction—I simply let it out me by implication. By reading this book, I've come out to you.

Now, whenever I write about anything involving gay things (including myself), I feel like I'm channeling that seven-year-old, the one who had the balls to proudly and effortlessly declare his sexuality and shout, "I'm gay! I'm gay!" to the world and not give a shit who cared.

A CASE OF JEFF

I remember that time you told me you said
"Love is touching souls"
Surely you touched mine
'Cause part of you pours out of me
In these lines from time to time
- Joni Mitchell, "A Case of You"

I first met Jeff for four minutes.

On a cold December night, I was at a gay/lesbian speed-dating event hosted by the Vancouver Public Library. I was here primarily to find someone who could help me get over my ex, and I always wanted to try speed dating because it seemed both fun and funny. A few mildly interesting dates in, the blond guy who I first saw sitting by himself before the night started, avoiding everyone's glances, now sat in front of me. He was wearing a wool sweater, and his hair was so blond it was almost white. With his day-old scruff and dark eyes, he resembled William Powell in *My Man Godfrey*—as the Forgotten Man (homeless man), not the well-groomed butler he transforms into later in the film.

"Hi!" I chimed, offering a casual smile.

"Hi," he flatly replied.

Everyone had been given pseudonyms that were related to LGBT characters or authors; his nametag read Dudley something. I was Ennis del Mar. When I explained that Ennis was played by Jake Gyllenhaal in *Brokeback Mountain* and died in the end, Dudley promptly corrected me.

"That was Heath Ledger. Jake Gyllenhaal played Jack Twist. Ennis was the one who lived," he lectured tonelessly.

"Oh. Oh yeah, right."

At this special speed-dating event, termed "Read Dating," singles were encouraged to bring their favourite book, movie, or CD as a conversation starter instead of awkwardly staring at each other in uncomfortable silence. So, I asked him about the CD he had brought; he was the only person I met that night who had brought one. He told me a bit about the artist, who was British, and I told him a bit about my DVD, *The Apartment*, my favourite movie. As I spoke with him, his blue-grey eyes bore into me, seemingly attentive, while the rest of his face registered indifference, as if I were reading the dictionary aloud in a monotone.

Just four minutes, I told myself. Finally, the bell rang and they called for us to move on. We exchanged rather curt goodbyes, and Dudley got up to leave. As the next guy sat down in front of me and started talking, Dudley, instead of moving on, stood a few feet away, scribbling something on his sheet of paper for a little too long. Obviously, he had written more than a simple Y or N next to my name. I didn't care though, since I would never see him again.

I never learned what it was he wrote about me.

A few days later, my friend Brian sent me a message on Facebook, asking if I had gone to Read Dating; attached to the message was a picture of his friend, who also attended. I recognized him instantly.

Yeah, of course I remember him, I replied.

His name is Jeff, Brian told me. Jeff.

***

A couple weeks later, Brian invited me to a (non-sexual) dip in the hot tub in his apartment building (emphasis on non-sexual, seriously) and invited a couple friends too. Not only had the recent reconciliation with my ex failed, but I also found out he was seeing someone who was living halfway around the world, in Japan, for eight months. This only made me feel more insecure about myself. He would rather be with someone who wasn't in the country—or the same continent— than to be with me, who had changed and was ready to work things out. I felt worthless. For days and days, I moped and sobbed at home, or I moped and secretly sobbed at work, so Brian's invitation seemed like a good excuse to do something besides mope and sob. He said I knew both his friends who were coming: Michael, whom I had previously met, and a blond guy who was "also quiet and introverted."

Still completely oblivious, I imagine Brian rolling his eyes as he texted, *It's Jeff.*

What?! This is going to be so awkward! I scream-texted him.

It's only awkward if you make it awkward.

Perhaps it was the hot water, but surprisingly, conversation was easy. I sat across the Jacuzzi from Jeff and learned he was a few years older than me. He was a social worker but had a master's in Music Technology. We chatted about how he knew Brian and Michael, and about what happened after Read Dating. No one had contacted him after that night, he confessed. When I asked if he wanted to know what I thought of him when we met that night, he said sure.

"I thought you were completely disinterested in everything I had to say." Jeff's laughter echoed throughout the cavernous room.

"People think I'm a snob when I meet them. I just... don't know what to say. And I don't like it." He looked away, gazing at the bubbling water for several seconds. We sat there in comfortable, compatible silence, me watching him stare off at nothing.

That's when I recognized it: he was thinking, removing himself from reality and swimming in the sea of his thoughts and ideas. If his process was anything like mine, he might have been pondering all the different times he was too quiet with a date or reliving the four-minute chats with the men from Read Dating. Besides myself, I had never seen anyone else do the same thing, the exact same way. I thought I was the only one.

Afterward, the four of us went to get some food at a near-empty restaurant on Davie Street. While they prattled on about people and events which I had no idea about, at times, Jeff blurted out a few things, added bits and pieces to the story, then relapsed into silence, gazing off again at something. Suddenly, a spark went off in my brain, and I quickly scanned the faces around the table. I glanced wide-eyed at Brian who was busy telling a story about his last trip, and then at Michael, who was listening and smiling.

Why can't they see what I'm seeing?

I can understand people fairly well right off the bat. I can see their layers. Most people are uninteresting to me because they lay their thoughts, their character out so easily, so openly. They show their cards without hesitation. Those I find interesting or cool, I want to get to know quickly and be around them a lot.

In that moment, I realized Jeff was different. I could see layers behind him, but I didn't know what they were. Clearly, he was someone who I knew wasn't saying everything on his mind. He was someone I wanted to get to know slowly, purposefully. Deeply.

I snapped out of it when they asked me if I wanted to go to a New Year's party at another friend's house. I told them I wasn't much into parties.

"It'll be fun," they all said. I looked at Jeff, who was looking back at me. I told them I might go.

***

I want to kiss Jeff at midnight. I don't know why. I genuinely just feel like it.

My phone vibrated in my pocket; Brian's response to my text was that of surprise, but he wished me luck.

A little more than a week and a short chain of messages from Jeff later, I strolled down Fraser Street, uncertain what to expect at this party. However, I could already sense that something, for better or for worse, was going to change between me and Jeff.

The music was shitty—some overproduced, generic top 40s fare—and too loud. Red plastic cups of various alcoholic beverages were on the floor, on tables, knocked over. People were shouting and stretching the vowels of their drunk laughs while playing beer pong. Much different from the board-games-and-juice parties I hosted at home.

I found Jeff reclining on the back porch smoking and drinking with friends. I didn't know he smoked. As the last minutes of the year ticked away, I saw Jeff periodically; the last time before midnight, he was sitting next to a guy named Josh, an unassuming young guy with blond hair who reminded me of a lamb, on the couch downstairs, bathed in the ethereal rainbow glow of Christmas lights strewn around the room. Jeff mentioned that Josh was going through some troubles and he wanted to be there for him. I understood but longed to sit with Jeff too.

Minutes to midnight, everyone crowded in the living room around the television and counted down as the previously aired telecast of the ball dropping in New York's Times Square played on TV.

"Happy New Year!" everyone screamed. Then we all hugged one another in a giant orgy of limbs and laughter. As Jeff came by and opened his arms, I found I couldn't kiss him. What if he didn't want to kiss me? I didn't want to make an ass of myself, and anyway, I was pretty sure he didn't want to kiss me. We ended up simply hugging and wishing each other a happy new year before he disappeared into the crowd again, leaving me with my disappointment.

As the first day of the year commenced, the house slowly emptied out, becoming eerily quieter and quieter. I was ready to go home too, as there really wasn't much to do, but I wanted to say goodbye to Jeff first. I found him upstairs, wandering around, looking lost. He seemed a bit emotional, but I couldn't quite pinpoint what it was or why. In a slightly slurred voice, he said he was getting ready to leave as well and was just getting his things, including a guitar-shaped cribbage board (I had never played cribbage and had no clue what a cribbage board looked like. So basically, I kept an eye out for something that resembled a guitar). We went downstairs and searched. Nothing.

As I followed him back up the carpeted stairs, he suddenly halted. His back still to me, Jeff made a choking noise, then burst into tears. After initial panic, I tried my best to calm and comfort him and decided it would be best to take him home, which was fortunately only a few blocks away.

A small group of friends from the party, including me, stayed with Jeff inside the dark of his little laneway house (we groped around the walls but failed to find the light switches) while he stopped and started crying. From what I gathered from Jeff and his friends, Josh, the guy he had tried to help earlier, made a hurtful, nasty comment to him.

Curled up in a fetal position on his couch, Jeff repeatedly mumbled, "I was just trying to help him..." I felt helpless and looked to his uncomfortable and equally helpless friends (except one who was giving Jeff the mother of all pep talks, mostly to no avail). The only thing I knew how to do was when he mumbled, "Hold me," to no one in particular, and I cradled him in my arms as he sobbed. When he more or less calmed down, the friends departed. I asked if he wanted me to stay; Jeff replied that it would be nice if I did. That was the first night I slept over at another guy's place, something I had waited years to do with the right person.

I slept on the bed (not *in* the bed) next to him as he drifted off. Late/early in the night, I woke up nearly frozen as I had no blanket or covers. Beside me, Jeff shuffled, awake.

"Jeff? I'm really cold. Do you mind if I come under the covers?"

"No."

That was all the answer I needed. I stripped down to my boxers and climbed into the warmth of the bed. We put our arms around each other, and it immediately felt right.

"You can touch me," Jeff murmured. My arm draped across his chest, I touched his side with my hand.

"I am touching you." He chuckled and moved my hand lower.

I said softly, "I don't want this to be something you'll regret."

I'm glad to have met you, Aaron, he texted me when we parted the morning after.

***

That first week of the new year, I saw Jeff almost every day. I told Brian excitedly that I wasn't used to seeing someone so much—even my previous boyfriends—but that it felt so good. The only thing was that I wasn't sure where things were between me and Jeff, which Brian helped bluntly clarify: "You're seeing each other." I let the words roll around in my head, and smiled to myself. Apparently, he and Josh had also made amends. I was wary of the news since Josh was the cause of Jeff's breakdown, but if it helped, I was all for it.

When I was with Jeff, it always felt so comfortable, so right to be with someone who I felt understood me in a way no one else did, like our mutual pleasure of silence. And in turn, I felt like I understood him, and recognized how special he was when no one else seemed to. Most nights, I just held him while we lay on the couch or in/on his bed, our arms and legs woven in and out of each other. Sometimes he put on a record from his vinyl collection, or the TV was on. I touched his skin, tracing my fingers along his lightly hairy arms, his chest, even his palms, as if my hands were erasers, healing over the scars. Eyes closed, smiling at my touch, he just talked while I listened, only adding my thoughts if he asked. Sex didn't happen much, and when it did, it was always me getting in his pants. Although I wished to be touched too, I never said a word about it.

This is about Jeff, not about me. I'm here to listen and help. I'll tell him about me when the time is right, when he asks, I told myself. *He's gone through a difficult experience.*

He makes the moves. I follow.

***

One night, after watching a movie together, we went for a walk down at the Canada Place waterfront. It was oddly but pleasantly still; virtually no one was around, and we joked that it was like a zombie apocalypse had occurred in Vancouver. After strolling and conversing a bit, all of a sudden, Jeff stopped walking and put his hands on my arms.

"Aaron, you're giving me so much medicine!"

He explained how, during a spiritual workshop he attended some years back, medicine didn't have to be physical—it was anything that could help you feel better. With that, he gave me a big hug and thanked me for being in his life.

"You know, you give me medicine too. Maybe not in the same way, but you do," I told him. He smiled, but never asked further. I never told him about how the simple act of being with him was the one and only activity, it seemed, that kept the constant barrage of negative thoughts of my ex and the past at bay, far, far away. I didn't tell him how, when a friend asked me how I was coping after the fallout with my ex, I responded, "Who?" With Jeff, I was always in the present, and with Jeff, the present was always good.

For once in my life, the present was simply good.

***

Our Greatest Hits:

"I have something for you." Jeff handed me a wallet-sized Polaroid. He was sitting in a chair, smiling, and he looked younger, despite the photo having been taken only a few days prior. I grinned and thanked him for the picture, put it in my wallet, and would show it to my friends after and gush about how special he was.

"I have a surprise for you too, actually." From my bag, I pulled out a package of Hershey's Hugs.

"Since I can't always be there to hug you, you can have a chocolate and imagine me hugging you."

Wilfred was on TV one night. Jeff said Elijah Wood was cute, while I argued that he was merely decent. I told Jeff he was way handsomer than Elijah, and of course, Jeff didn't believe me. When I got home that night, I posted a comment on Jeff's Facebook profile picture: *Elijah Wood has nothing on this handsome stud.*

While driving me home one night, Jeff suddenly interrupted me.

"Aaron, can I hold your hand?"

"Of course! Of course. You don't need to ask." He took my hand and drove me one-handedly back home while I suppressed the giddy feeling in me.

After finishing class at nearly 10pm one night, I took the #49 bus, then ran twenty blocks straight with my backpack on to Jeff's house. Panting slightly (thanks to my long-distance track and field experience) and very warm upon arrival, Jeff noted, "Aww, you ran to see me!" and chuckled.

I didn't know what to say, so I just smiled back.

While sitting across from each other on his couch, Jeff strummed his guitar and played a few songs. My favourite was his cover of Joni Mitchell's "A Case of You," which was also his favourite to play. As if denying there was an audience, he always played with eyes closed. His voice was soft, breathy. I was so used to serenading guys on the piano myself that it was only then that I knew how it felt to receive a song. I listened and watched in awe. When he was done, I leaned over and kissed him on the cheek.

"How did I know you were going to do that?" he said with a grin.

Once, while intertwined in each other's arms, Jeff asked me, "If you died today, what would be your greatest accomplishment?" I told him about the time I potentially saved someone's life. He was a friend—well, acquaintance—on Myspace, and had posted a public message saying he had taken some pills minutes ago and apologized to his family about his death. After about half an hour of freaking out and calling, I hung up with the authorities in Myrtle Beach, South Carolina, where my online friend lived, and a few days later, saw that he had logged in to Myspace and was alive. I don't know whether he was saved because of me or someone else.

"Wow. And I was gonna say my greatest accomplishment was getting a master's."

I didn't tell him I had been waiting a very long time for someone to save me, and that I might have found him.

Jeff lay on the couch with his t-shirt halfway up his torso and his dick, hard, out of his undone jeans.

I sat back and watched him, and the words formed easily in my head: *You are so beautiful.* If this were a photograph, I could live in it forever.

But instead of saying these words aloud, I swallowed them.

The night he gave me a kiss—a real kiss—before I left his place, I immediately texted Brian and told him. I tried to casually mention it to Jeff later in text.

He responded, "Oh, I usually kiss people goodbye."

My arms, under his shirt, were pressing him close to me. Sitting on the floor leaning against the couch where I was seated, Jeff reached up and stroked my hair. As we sat in silence, I thought about this guy—this goddamn special guy—who chose to spend his time with me, day after day. *Me.* No boyfriend had done that for me. And I wasn't even his boyfriend.

I couldn't help it; the thought made me tear up. When I sniffled, Jeff craned his neck around and looked up with inquiring eyes but said nothing. So I said nothing.

***

Hey, Jeff! How're you?

To be honest, not that well. I think I need to take a break from texting for a bit.

Okay. I'm sorry if I overwhelmed you with my texts. If there's anything I can do, let me know. I'll leave it up to you when you want to start talking again.

***

Brian told me I pestered Jeff with my texts, even though I tried my best to hold off. As we lost touch, the thoughts of my ex came back, stronger and more frequent than before. When I saw my ex around school, I had difficulty breathing and my heart rate spiked—minor anxiety attacks. I didn't feel like doing anything most of the time and I got sick often, which I attributed to my poor mental health. I discovered my comment on Jeff's profile picture had been deleted. He backed out of meeting my friends for dinner. Once, when spending time at his place, I felt he wanted me to leave, so I got dressed. When he came back from the bathroom, he was telling me, "You can stay over if you want—" then stopped when he saw me ready to go.

When I touched him, I didn't know if he wanted me to. His layers shrouded him once more.

***

I feel so screwed up, Aaron. I don't know if I want cuddles or hook-ups or what.

You're not screwed up. These things take time to figure out. If there's anything I can do to help, let me know.

***

On another night, Brian and I were reclining in some comfy chairs at the Fairmont Hotel downtown (of all places), chatting and hanging out.

"Last weekend, Jeff went to Spit. He didn't really want to

go, but I told him he should, and he met some other white dude there. They were making out for a while and then—"

"Sorry for interrupting, Brian. But could you please not tell me about Jeff and who he's..."

Brian studied me for a moment. "Yeah, of course."

***

The last time we were together, Jeff and I watched *The Apartment*, the movie I had brought to Read Dating months ago. During the film, I kept glancing at Jeff and suppressed as best I could the trembling inside me; I was terrified that I wanted to touch him but couldn't. The door to his bedroom was ajar, and I could see his mattress on the floor, covers unmade. Despite willing myself not to, I couldn't help but imagine Jeff and someone else cuddling and having sex in that bed.

At the end of the film, Shirley MacLaine realizes how sweet and caring Jack Lemmon has been to her the whole time, and sprints through the streets to see him on New Year's Day. After Jack professes his love for her, she playfully teases him to "Shut up and deal" the cards to their game, ending the film on a sweet note.

Jeff exclaimed, "Wow, harsh. What a bitch."

I looked over at him in silence.

***

While on vacation in Hong Kong, I somehow found myself listening to Adele's cover of Bob Dylan's "Make You Feel My Love." It was one of those songs that hit me in the gut, that I knew immediately was meant for my situation with Jeff. After listening to it on repeat for days, I vowed to learn the song and sing it to Jeff. I was going to show him how I felt.

There were times when I teared up just rehearsing the song at home. If anyone would understand the emotions of music, it would be Jeff.

One night, at the local movie theatre where I worked, I was cashing out of my till near the end of my shift. I retrieved my phone, which I used as a calculator, and saw that Jeff had responded to my message (*Hey Jefferson Airplane. How're you?*) I had sent him earlier that day. I put the till on the cash-out table and opened the message.

Jeff said he needed to be honest: he was in a relationship now, with someone across the border. He told me he didn't think it was a good idea for the two of us to hang out together anymore; he hoped I was well, and that I would understand.

I put the phone down on the table and stared at it until the screen went black. I simply sat there and stared at nothing for several minutes, aware of every breath I was taking, feeling the heat rise in my face. As my vision got blurrier and blurrier, I noticed the dents and cracks on the table. The table, which must have been new at one point, had been used day after day, carelessly banged, kicked, and pounded on. Beaten.

Then the tears rolled down my face, dissolving all the thoughts and words I would never say and sing to Jeff.

I will always feel like our time together amounted to a moment of sitting across from each other at a table at the library on a cold winter's night.

I will always feel like four minutes was all we had.

TRUE OR FALSE

I used to imagine you from time to time after you stopped thinking of me. I don't remember why I did it. It rose up from the waters, a shipwreck dredged from the depths of my insecure mind. Whenever I wound the film reel through the projector in my head, it felt like incendiary light quietly burning, eating the final frames of celluloid. Is a fantasy still considered a fantasy if it's negative? Should it be a nightmare, even when I'm awake?

In my head, it was a Hollywood production: fade in to well-lit, soft yellow light you could almost reach out and caress. You were in bed, the stringy curls of your hair matted on pillows as large and fluffed as barrels. Skin melding with silk bed sheets, a big puffy duvet engulfing your small frame in a warm hug, something my skinny body could never quite do. Eyes closed. Sleepy puffs slipping through parted lips.

The camera pulls back, inch by inch. A hand reaches into frame, followed by trails of arm hair. The hand lingers over your face for a second as if hesitating to touch such divine beauty, then drifts down and thumb-strokes your cheek. Eyelids flutter open, pupils adjust, irises radiate cedar bark-brown. Slow like the reveal of invisible ink, a drowsy smile appears, one that murmurs, *I'm glad to be with here with you.*

Pulling back still. Reveal a large bed, wooden headboard. The hair on the arm snakes up and up, connecting to a toned bicep, a muscled shoulder. Palm dips underneath the sheets and roams the contours of your body. Then, camera pulling back just a bit further until finally: a face. It is never distinguishable, never the same; but it is always white, classically good-looking, and usually boasts a neatly trimmed beard. And right on cue—there's that mirrored smile on his face now too; perhaps this one whispers, *You are so beautiful and you are mine.* You smell of him: of man, sweat from the gym mixed with sharply sweet cologne. And he smells of you: briny seawater. It makes him want to lick you, taste you on his tongue.

Hold the frame. His hand is back up, cradling your head. It is all too much, he cannot fight it anymore—suddenly, his lips are on yours. Yours on his. All eyes are hidden. Breathe each other in, breathe yourselves in. Strings swell, fireworks ignite, curtain closes. Fade to black. Credits roll ("Thanks to all those who made this possible").

House lights go up.

Me, alone in the theatre, and now I must deal with this ripping of flesh inside my stomach and my eyes that want to drown themselves. Heave some air into my lungs. Tell myself that it wasn't real. It's only me letting my worst fears abduct me and take me joyriding while I sit helplessly strapped in the back. I constantly let my mind cliff-dive into unseen oceans when the truth was unknown but out there at the same time. A movie I had yet to watch.

You told me you didn't have time to love. So, this was all false, just another forgettable summer flick. This couldn't be a reality.

It couldn't possibly be true. Of course not.

No.

But it was.

THE MAN IN THE ARENA

I am in the yellow-tiled kitchen, searching for a snack. Mom and Dad aren't here. A piece of paper lays on the kitchen counter, and being the curious child I am, I look. It's a note, written in my father's scrawl. Part of it is in Chinese, which I can't read. But the part I can read is understandable to me, even at my young age.

"I hope we can work things out," he writes. "I love you."

Something else catches my eye. Beside the kitchen counter is the garbage can. Something—or rather, several things—are in there that don't look like garbage.

Roses. Several long-stemmed red roses.

I don't remember much from my childhood, but I remember this vividly.

***

As far back as I can recall, I have been a romantic. There is no other way to explain something that feels so natural to me, like knowing I am an artist or that I am gay.

Part of what supported this belief was romantic comedies, which I watched from an early age. As a structural rule in rom-coms, the couple always breaks up (some for reasons dumber and more forced than others), but they always manage to work through it, usually via some big, winning-back spectacle. In *Music and Lyrics*, Hugh Grant's character finally writes his own lyrics and sings his new song in front of an arena full of people, which includes the girlfriend he recently broke up with. Harry sprints countless blocks to a New Year's Eve party and declares all the reasons he has loved Sally as more than a friend-who-happens-to-be-a-girl (while Frank Sinatra croons in the background) in *When Harry Met Sally*... I don't know why, but I never questioned any of this. As far as I knew, people actually chased their exes down, admitted their faults and wrong-doings, and got back together because it was simply supposed to happen that way. It all felt like things I would do. It all seemed logical.

To many, winning someone back is an admission of fault. Relationships almost always involve power dynamics, and when a couple breaks up, the dynamics may appear more evident than before. Winning someone back could be viewed as being weak, as needing the other person.

But in her Ted Talk "Listening to shame," author and vulnerability researcher Brené Brown notes that although many people believe being vulnerable is a weakness, she defines it as "emotional risk, exposure, uncertainty... Vulnerability is our most accurate measurement of courage."

Attempting to reconcile with an ex-lover and knowing that things may not happen the way you want is being vulnerable—and courageous. However, not everyone sees it this way.

Sam was my first boyfriend when I was nineteen years old. He told me he wasn't out (while I was) but I thought I could live with this because I cared deeply about him and believed he was worth it. Despite this, after nearly four months of being introduced to his friends and family as a friend, Sam told me one night that he would never come out were he to remain in Vancouver. When we tried to talk things out, it seemed clear that things were done; I couldn't be a hidden part of someone's life forever.

Yet, I still had feelings for him, and genuinely felt like things between us were not finished. Upon dwelling on our relationship for several weeks, I met with him one day to talk.

In my mind, the logic was all there. There was no reason for him to say no; I came to the realization that I didn't need him to come out to anyone. I only wanted him to consider it, and then we could slowly work through it.

"I can't see myself going down that path," he told me. I left feeling defeated.

It was only after the end of my second relationship with G. that I became self-aware enough to realize my own process of winning someone back. Inadvertently, I found myself sifting through the almost ten months' worth of memories, recalling words and events: receiving a poem he wrote to me when we had begun dating; my nervously choking out "I love you" for the first time to someone and crying when he echoed it back; all the times we had sex and felt a deep connection between us. Compared to Sam, I felt he was my first true boyfriend.

I pored over every minute detail, analyzing everything, a habit which I attribute to all the English courses I had taken, having to pick apart details and examine them in essays. But this wasn't simply rumination. It didn't dawn on me until later but I was subconsciously analyzing everything in order to find a solution to a problem that I always felt was solvable. All because I loved him.

With G., the solution came half a year later. It was partly because I had imposed my schedule of when I wanted to see him and had ended up feeling sad and neglected, instead of working on a schedule together. The stupidity I felt when I realized this—that this was the answer to such a simple problem that had broken us apart—was overwhelming.

For me, winning someone back is not about saying I was wrong. In fact, it has never been that at all. I always thought that winning someone back was a foolproof way of showing your love, and in part, by also being vulnerable.

Some people don't believe that a person can truly change. But if you have found a solution or learned how to make the relationship better or truly changed as a person, is this not enough to earn someone back? Let me put it this way: if a car you've had for years breaks down, but is fixed and upgraded with new, better parts, considering all the time, energy, and memories you've spent on it, would you not stick with the car?

***

Why is there such a disconnect between winning people back in movies and popular culture and in reality? Perhaps it is the fact that movies are only fantasies—that's why we pay to watch them; they don't happen in the real world. Or maybe the real world is much less romantic than we think or want it to be. Or more likely, I don't have friends who would win someone back.

My friend Lily once told me that her brother believed that once a couple had broken up, they should never expect to get back together. Once broken, broken forever.

When she told me this, I didn't understand. It felt like someone telling me the Earth was flat, or that I wanted to be a doctor when I grow up, or that golf is cool. I couldn't understand ever thinking like that. But if people believed this, it would mean people don't win others back. It would mean people dismiss movies as typical Hollywood endings—who, in my eyes, simply give up months and years they spent with someone they loved.

Maybe it is only women who want to be won back. After all, statistically, they are the ones who watch rom-coms and believe in them (with the exception of myself, it seems). Hollywood films feature straight couples messing things up, with the man usually proclaiming his love to his female love interest in the end. Is this, perhaps, more of an expectation of heterosexual relationships?

My father may not have been a very good parent, having been absent for most of his children's lives, but I will say that he was tenacious. Years after my parents' separation, my father asked my mother if they could work things out, for the kids; she agreed, albeit hesitantly. Sometimes my father came over to our house and sat at the kitchen table while we silently walked around this familiar stranger. Other times he asked me to invite my mom out to lunch together and talk with him. And other instances, he simply called, wishing to talk to her. I wonder if he was influenced at all by what was expected of him or if he wanted to do it of his own volition.

After G. and I broke up, I wrote a song about/for him and then performed it live at a show. In addition to telling him how hurt I felt upon our break-up, I sang about being willing to "wait for [his] golden epiphany." I uploaded the video online and sent him the link, telling him I wanted him to watch it. A few days later, he replied, saying things would not change if we got back together.

I was more than willing to at least try to win someone back that I loved. Brian didn't seem to understand it, however. "Why do you keep doing that?" he asked, confused. I tried to explain my rationale but he still didn't seem to get it.

"Would you ever try to win someone back?" I asked.

He pondered this. "I haven't been in that situation, so I don't know if I would." His response, like Lily's brother's view that couples break up forever, puzzled me. Perhaps winning someone back is not part of gay culture. Why win someone back if no other gay guy is doing it? After a split, some gay men go right back into the dating game or have tons of re-bound sex. This would explain why I have always felt ashamed to be a romantic gay guy when other men out there don't seem to give a damn.

It is a realization that is both enlightening and disheartening.

***

There is such an overrepresentation of winning people back and succeeding that the possibility of it not working out doesn't seem to exist. When the lead couple in *(500) Days of Summer* predictably falls apart, Tom vows, "I don't want to get over her. I want to get her back." So, he sets off figuring out his life. When they meet again sometime later, he discovers that she is engaged, and plunges into depression, drinking, and going to the drugstore to buy Twinkies in his bathrobe.

Spoiler alert: they don't get back together in the end.

I commend this film for at least trying to break the predictable mould of typical rom-coms. There should be more films like this. Rejection occurs daily, and I want to see it.

Although I was always unclear about my parents' history and the reasons for their separation, I knew, based on the way she mentioned him as well as her stubbornness, that my mom would never change her mind about him. Despite agreeing to try and work things out, her attitude barely changed, and she continued to be cold and curt to him on the phone and in-person. It never occurred to me that there was anything my dad could do to win her back. I never had an opinion of what he was doing, but I wondered if he knew that it was all futile. Rejection occurred all the time for him, yet he still soldiered on, undaunted.

I feel that people underestimate just how difficult it is to be rejected, and in this case, to lose when it comes to winning someone back. Upon figuring out the solution to the break-up with G., we met on a cold December afternoon, days after his birthday, and a few before mine. Eventually, after walking in silence for a while and uncertain how to begin, I blurted everything out. He was unusually quiet but listened attentively. He told me that when he was with me, he didn't know what he wanted, and he still didn't. When I told him about what I had figured out, he said it made sense, but offered nothing else.

Finally, I told him I didn't want to be the one asking him back, as I had previously attempted and been turned down.

"So, since you don't know what you want, I assume you're not seeing anyone," I ventured.

He looked over at me. "Just because I don't know what I want, why should that mean I'm not seeing anyone?"

Everything in my body wrenched. I knew I should stop, that this was heading down a dark road to somewhere from which I wouldn't be able to return. But I couldn't help it. I needed to know. I made myself vulnerable and asked the question that would affect me for years to come.

"Okay. So are you seeing someone?"

"Kind of."

The two words were trapped in my ears, ricocheting wildly. They eventually became words I would avoid using for several months after. In that moment, everything became slow. My face and neck burned and it became difficult to breathe. My heart rate spiked. I felt something rupture and spill inside me. My body suddenly became too much for my legs to support, and they wobbled as we continued walking. I mumbled that I needed to sit down as a wave of nausea hit me; I barely managed to suppress the urge to vomit.

For several minutes, I sat on a bench and gasped for air, like breathing through a straw, and stared down at my trembling hands in my lap. I sensed him sitting next to me, but he did nothing. It was only when I became aware of myself and what was going on that I was finally able to calm down. We talked a bit more after, but there wasn't much else to say. I had lost. But I lost more than I knew.

Much like Tom in *(500) Days*, I became depressed. I sobbed in my room for days, my body heaving up and down while I sniffled and choked on my breath. Sad music became my only playlist, and I replayed the same film clip from *The Broken Hearts Club*, where one of the characters declares his love to his ex-boyfriend after his ex is seeing someone new, only to make myself cry more. Though I had been of legal drinking age for a few years, I never liked alcohol, but I bought some for the first time and drank vodka straight from the bottle alone at home.

The next time I saw my ex, at the start of the next semester at school, he was walking up to the bus stop. Immediately, my pulse jumped, and I gasped short puffs of air, much like before. Though I had to take the same bus, I found I couldn't physically be near him. Ultimately, I turned down the street in the opposite direction, taking a different route home. This physical reaction happened every time I saw him at school, which, thankfully, was seldom.

I found out later online that I had symptoms of anxiety, triggered by my ex's revelation. I had developed anxiety—the actual medical condition, not the casual, everyday meaning—from attempting to win someone back and losing, something I had never expected could happen. Memories which had once kept me hopeful now haunted and hurt me every day; my poor mental health lowered my immune system, and I became sick frequently for longer periods. When a friend mentioned that G.'s new interest was living in Japan for eight months, my self-worth evaporated. I felt undesirable, like trash. This was all because I was vulnerable, because I believed my ex and I could get back together.

I was not prepared for an outcome like this because I never saw it anywhere. Perhaps the reason we don't see more representations of events like developing physical medical conditions, not merely mental, after failing to win someone back in media is because this is not something people want (or pay) to watch, like depressing news stories. It would certainly shatter the glass ceiling of traditional romantic comedies, although it would make the film unromantic and not very funny. Ignorance is bliss. But should it be?

You would think this would put me off talking to my ex again. And yet, I went on to ask him again months later, only to lose.

Again. And again.

It got to the point that G., in his final email, said, "Please don't try to win me back, because I will have to hurt you if you do."

***

Being the one asked back is being in a position of control—it comes back to power dynamics. An acquaintance of mine and her steady boyfriend broke up. She recalled that, about a week later, he contacted her and asked her back. When she told me this, she remarked, "Yeah, that's right. You're gonna come back," and laughed.

I wondered about this. Was she laughing because she perceived him to need her more than she needed him? Did she expect him to ask her back? Or did she perceive herself to be in control, to be wanted?

I think back to when I received that text a week after breaking up with G., telling me there were some things he wanted to talk to me about. I smiled and swelled with joy. To me, the only thing he could possibly tell me was that he wanted to get back together. It felt wonderful to be desired. It reassured the insecure part of me that for years had told me I wasn't worth anyone's love (he didn't end up asking me back that day, only wanted to talk about our relationship).

And for my mother, did she view my father and his persistence as a nuisance, like a puppy relentlessly jumping on her leg and yipping, wanting attention each time he reached out to fix their relationship? He had plainly told her before that he wished to make amends and though she had agreed, she remained quite hostile towards him.

I never thought winning someone back could be unwanted. It's like turning someone down if they proposed. Everyone says yes. Or at least everyone is supposed to.

***

Friends readily come to the aid of the brokenhearted because it is their duty, their role as supporting characters, to ensure that the couple get back together. They intervene, give stirring, angry, and/or emotional monologues, provide times and dates when the ex-love will be at the airport for their departing flight. Always there for their friends and because the love story is the A-plot, friends are the players ready to hurry things along for the lead couple's inevitable reunion and happily ever after. I think something about the spectacle and pressure of having multiple people believe you should be together with someone has an influence on these eventual happy endings.

The last time I tried to win back G., even after failing previously, I wrote a thinly veiled story on my blog about a man's experience grieving his ex. In the second to last chapter, the main character writes a letter outlining all the things he is sorry about, followed by what he learned and how he is going to be a better person and boyfriend, all of which doubled as things I meant in real life. I sent the link of the story to my and G.'s mutual friends, asking them to help me pass it on to G. and make him understand.

I thought for sure they would help me out. Not only that, but they would go the extra mile to ensure we got back together, preferably in a super-romantic way. Instead, only one of them responded. She advised me to write things out in a letter, not a public blog, which she would be willing to deliver to G.

When I met her with my handwritten letter, she told me bluntly, "I think it's over." I immediately wanted to shut her up: *I didn't ask for your opinion. I just need you to do this for me. What kind of friend are you?*

But that's the thing. We expect friends to just do what we want, rather than give us a reality check.

She still delivered the letter. I still failed. She was right.

As for my other friends, my best friend told me she didn't know what to do with the link I sent her. She wanted to help, but thought a random message from a former acquaintance wouldn't be effective. Maybe the rest of my friends were too busy or didn't care enough that I was trying to win back someone I loved. Or perhaps they didn't think we should be together.

When I was eleven, my mother arranged rides for me and my sister, Maggie, to our new school with Mr. Yan, a widower and a physiotherapist. His daughter Jessica had been my friend since the second grade, and since we lived nearby and now attended the same school, it seemed natural and easier for one parent to drive the three of us than separately. Apart from the organizing of who was going to drive which days, my mother and Mr. Yan didn't converse about much else; at most, there may have been some occasional chit-chat about school, comparing their children's progress.

When we kids, now teens, entered high school, rides were no longer needed since we attended different schools. Around the same time, my parents separated; my father moved out and back in with my grandparents. My mom, meanwhile, continued communicating with Mr. Yan.

From time to time, during our brief, stilted conversations, my father occasionally inquired, "Does Maggie still hang out with Jessica?"

When I told him that she did, he responded, "Does your mom still talk to Jessica's dad?" Sometimes she did, I replied, but usually to find out if he knew the whereabouts of my oft-disappearing and difficult-to-reach sister.

"I need you to do something for me." His small beady eyes glanced down to the table. "Don't let them get together," he said, unashamed to hide the jealousy and fear in his voice.

For one, I was not the least bit concerned of the possibility that my mom and Mr. Yan might start dating. I knew their relationship was platonic, nothing more than being fellow parents, and anyway, witnessing my mother's disinterest in my father—really, all men—it was unlikely she would be interested in anyone again, much less Mr. Yan.

But more importantly, I did not know what I had to do with what was going on between them. The way I saw it, it was none of my business what my mother was doing. Aside from a frightening incident while driving the three of us to school one day when he yelled obscenities at another driver and gave them the finger (they yelled back too), he didn't seem like a terrible person.

Why should my father be with my mother? Did he deserve to be with her? Or was it simply because he was my father and she my mother, so they should be together, especially since they had been married for so long? I didn't know. I didn't feel like it was obvious the way it was portrayed in movies and books. I'm not sure I ever recall my mother and father having a special moment together, one where I thought, *They belong together*.

Perhaps my dad and I are the irritating exes, the flawed jerks that are constantly getting in the way of the true romance between the two clear lovers. It may be destiny for them, not for us.

I always assumed I was the main character of the story, but perhaps I have been the secondary character all along, the one who exists as catalyst for change and then is never heard from again, now irrelevant and unimportant.

***

"Why do you keep trying to win people back?" Brian asked me one day.

The answer seemed obvious. "Because I feel like there's always a chance. I'm constantly thinking of solutions subconsciously. I just feel like if we're both alive, there's always possibility," I responded.

"Because there's always hope."

That's what it comes down to, doesn't it? It's the one thing someone trying to win back the love of another person is hanging on to. The hope that they will say yes. Hope drives us on, in anything we do. We hope that it doesn't rain today. We hope that after we graduate from university, we will land a good job. We hope our lives turn out well.

But hope expires too. When G. told me he was seeing someone, it immediately killed any hope of us getting back together. I tried several times to talk with Sam until I finally gave up on him.

"You gotta give 'em hope," Harvey Milk famously quipped.

You gotta give 'em limited hope, I say.

***

In the next ten years following his separation, my father continued to try and talk with my mother. In the end, he offered one final deal: he wanted to move back in with my mother, my sister, and me, and to work things out between all of us. For our family. Otherwise, he would consider a divorce. When he called my grandmother and asked for her opinion, she informed him, "You're too late. If you had asked last year when we all went on the cruise to Alaska together, there might have been a chance."

Later, I overheard my mother rant to my grandmother, "It has taken him more than ten years and only now he wants to try working things out? It's just too late." My mother responded to his offer with silence—a wordless rejection. And so, my father finally let go.

In the same Ted Talk about vulnerability and shame, Brené Brown quotes an analogy from Teddy Roosevelt called "the man in the arena": "It is neither the critic nor the man who sits and points out what happens who counts. It is the man in the arena, who is covered in blood and sweat, is bruised and battered, who is the best when he wins. And when he loses, he does it greatly."

It is easier to agree with this than to believe it. Like my father, I was unsuccessful in my many attempts of reconciliation. I wish I could say that it was enough to have tried, so this would have a better ending, that this essay would conform to the design of a narrative arc, much like a romantic comedy. But after being pummeled round after round, after developing crippling anxiety, after seeing my father on his knees—I feel I have lost a great deal instead of losing greatly.

During an episode of *Glee*, Emma, Will's wife, fled their wedding ceremony. His friend and former student Finn advised a mopey Will, "This is, like, in the third act of the movie where the heartbroken guy chases through the crowded city streets to win his girl back. And then he does some big romantic gesture and the music swells—and then the crowd applauds and their eyes well up with tears. And then she'll take you back. That's just the way it works."

Without thinking, I found myself shouting at the screen. "You liar! Liar! Liar..."

IN THE DUST

OWEN and I have been messaging each other for a while when it sneaks up on me and pounces again. *Do you like cuddling, Owen?*

Yes, very much so. But, I've got a guy I've met that I'd like to take a serious shot with (too slow!:-P). I'd still love to meet up with you but as friends only. Is that ok?

Suddenly, I am digging and digging and furiously trying to bury that boiling in my stomach again, threatening to surface. I attempt to soothe it with some words.

I understand. Yes, that's fine. It just means you have to try and not fall in love with me when we meet. :)

The words are so kind, so behaved, so bullshit to me that I wonder if it makes him doubt them for a second.

Lol does that happen often?

No, I want to say, what you just did is all that ever happens.

With that, I sense a burst within me, twisting and winding my guts like a taffy puller machine. And I feel him, I watch him walk away. Ahead.

Imagine sitting inside a large university lecture hall filled with students writing an important exam. You have been studying for quite some time, and it's a good thing: it is supposed to be a challenging test, and the questions live up to it. Before writing a response, you scrutinize every word of the question with great care, pausing to double-, triple-, quadruple-check your answer. The exam is supposed to take three hours, and it appears you'll need every second since it's several pages, several sections long.

Five minutes in, you hear the scuffling of shoes and look up to see someone strolling confidently up to the front, handing in their test. *That's strange*, you think. You return to your work, but as you continue, you watch more and more people adding to the stack of papers on the desk even though the test only started a few minutes ago. Outside the doors, you can hear the muffled laughter and the murmurs of your classmates joking about the exam. The classroom inexorably empties out, leaving you as one of the last students left, and then *the* last, and you still have pages upon pages of questions remaining.

Most people have probably felt something similar to this, whether it was for an actual exam, school, jobs, or simply in life: your friend who started university with you is now graduating. You are switching majors yet again, and noticing that you are the oldest student in your classes. You have been sifting through endless customer-service job postings while your cousin continues to climb up the corporate ladder at their company. A sister announces her engagement to her gorgeous fiancé; you continue swiping through Tinder profiles on the daily for the next regrettable one-night stand. It's anxiety, it's frustration, it's queasiness, it's urgency, all in one. It is the feeling of being left behind while everyone around you advances; for the most part, it is difficult to not let it wash over you and consume you as you rush to catch up.

Reading Owen's text is not the first time I have felt it, this swelling in my gut that churns in me and often erupts in sadness. It happens when Vince casually mentions he is now living with his boyfriend in New West; it happens when Liam suggests it's not a good idea to cuddle because he is seeing someone; it happens when I bump into Mark on the bus and he tells me he has just come from his boyfriend's place. I feel as if they have bypassed me and have ascended to some higher plane, where love is abundant and it's a wonderful life. Meanwhile, I struggle to get a date with a decent guy my age who isn't overly concerned how masculine I may or may not be.

Media constantly reinforces that love is important in life, particularly for heterosexual, cisgender girls and women, and not only in romantic comedies like *Bridget Jones's Diary* either: the young women in several of Jane Austen's novels rush to find a suitor before they are deemed too old. Endless reality dating shows like *The Bachelor* feature multiple women vying for the affections of a classically handsome man who is supposed to give them their happily-ever-after; a study carried out by Jonathan W. Roberti in 2007 for the New College of Florida found that the majority of those who watched reality dating shows were young, single women.[15]

A woman without love wilts like a flower without sun, goes the proverb. And of course, society and families subtly (or sometimes not so subtly) emphasize finding a partner through arranged marriages, setting them up on dates, and parents inquiring every time you visit them, "You're how old

15 Jonathan W. Roberti, "Demographic Characteristics and Motives of Individuals Viewing Reality Dating Shows," *The Communication Review* 10, (2007): 117–134. https://doi.org/10.1080/10714420701350403.

now? When're you finally gonna get married?", all in an effort to redirect their fates as hideous, wrinkled spinsters, forever alone with their seventeen cats, like aging Miss Havisham in *Great Expectations* (minus the cats, although she may as well have had them). Despite a recent reclamation of the term "spinster" and with more and more women choosing not to follow what many consider outdated conventions, people still face and succumb to this pressure.

My friend Bekki is this one of such women. She may not admit it, but it is obvious to me from the way she's detailed her wedding plans and decided on her future kids' names that love is important to her (for the record, I don't think there is any shame in admitting this). Back when she was single, her face and voice lit up when she recounted pleasant dates. But it really became evident when, in response to a friend getting married, Bekki lamented on Facebook how she had correctly bet she would be the last of her friends to tie the knot. When my sister told her she was being overdramatic, Bekki dismissed her.

Although I thought her post was silly because, for one, I was not yet married either (or remotely close), I identified with how she felt. Every time I find out someone is living the narrative I so desperately crave for myself, it makes me stop, reevaluate my life and my choices. My thoughts become irrational. I cling to the notion that love is out there—but only as a limited-time offer. The "good ones" pair up early on and the longer it takes you to partner up, the faster your chances diminish. Pessimism seizes me: I am doing something wrong—how else to explain why I keep losing? Something has to change, something must give, but I have no indication what or how. The only thing I know is what I am currently do-ing—reaching out on apps and online dating sites with slight variations of the same opening line—so I continue doing that, until the cycle repeats itself all over again and I reexamine myself with greater desperation.

One day, years from now, if I have a mental breakdown from all this, I cannot say that I will be surprised. No, I expect it to happen.

As another classmate finishes their exam and strolls past you to the exit, you glance up and take notice of the clock hanging on the wall up at the front. The second hand jerks forward again and again, the incessant, insistent tick-tock rattling you more and more as you keep dwelling on it. You are sure you can finish in time—everyone does, right?—but then it dawns on you: what if you don't? There is no make-up test, no time extension. Once you're done, you're done. With that, you turn your attention back to the never-ending exam in front of you, a newfound, weighted stress now looming over every hastily scribbled response.

Depictions of young, beautiful people finding love are ev-erywhere; less common are those featuring older people doing the same, as if implying it doesn't exist or they don't exist. In society, there is a notion (again, more so for women than men) that love is a race against time. This belief traces back to when families attempted to find a suitor for their daughter before society judged her to be too old, stale goods. Women had a limited amount of time to find someone or else they passed a non-specific age, around the time they could no longer have kids was usually the case, and thus became undesirable. The only company you would be able to keep is your friends who flaunt their spouses in your face whilst displaying an obscene amount of public affection.

Between 1800 and 1900, the average age of marriage for women in the US was between twenty and twenty-two; in Britain, it was as young as sixteen. Throughout history, finding a husband was less about love and more about finance and livelihood; men provided income and a home, the two necessities in life at the time. Of course, that has changed vastly. Women are independent and have their own careers and can choose not to have children if they don't want any, but it seems this belief that people have expiry dates has lingered to the present.

I am aware that I do not face the same pressure of these expectations because there is much less of it directed at men to find a mate (apart from that time everybody was on George Clooney's case for being a bachelor, it seemed). Sure, men were expected to produce kids and have a family, but it is much less relevant now, especially, again, in the West. Instead, there are more images of men and sex today than love—in the countless TV shows, films, and songs where a man has an affair, or his frat bros celebrate him hooking up, for instance. If anything, fifty-year old single men come off to many as gay (I wasn't the only one thinking—nay, praying—Clooney was gay, right?).

It is no wonder I align myself more with women's expectations of finding love than men's. I think part of it is being able to relate more, like the quest to locate a man who doesn't have a pile of rocks for a brain (which is also a giant hurdle dating gay men, it seems).

Instead of society pressuring me, I pressure myself. From an early age, I knew I was meant to love. Perhaps it is simply the result of all the happily-ever-after gay teen novels I consumed and the romantic comedies I watched, but I know I was born to love the same way a hockey player claims he was born to play the sport, or a woman instinctually knows she wants to be a mother. Love—like hockey and motherhood for our would-be examples—becomes my goal. I study it. I learn it. I train for it. I have a physical list of fun/interesting first-date activities. I give personalized gifts to my significant others that they would love (for example, my last boyfriend once mentioned he never played Pokémon growing up, so I bought him a Gameboy Colour and Pokémon Red for Christmas because life is incomplete without having played Pokémon). I have taken boyfriends out and cooked them meals at home. I have serenaded boys on the piano, dedicated songs to them, written them poems. I have been patient and understanding if they are in the closet or are dealing with other personal issues. And of course, I (try to) pay attention to what turns them on in bed. I can say with confidence that I know how to be a damn good boyfriend.

What I want is someone to come home to, someone I can be ridiculous with and also have an intellectual conversation with, someone who looks at me when I am grey and grumpy and thinks, "Fuck, I love this bastard!" Since my teens, I have harboured a secret fantasy (don't worry, it's not sexual). It involves my older self, reading in bed while Norah Jones croons a jazz ditty in the background. My boyfriend/husband climbs in next to me and we chat for a bit, fill each other in on our mundane days. We kiss, turn off the lamp on the nightstand, and go to sleep. It's likely not the kind of fantasy you were imagining, but rather a scene straight out of a movie, I know. Something about it continues to profoundly resonate with me, despite years of hooking up, rejection, jadedness, and having a pitiable dating life.

Also, during my teenage years, when I started longing for a boyfriend (or really, another gay person to talk to), I felt left behind. Seeing straight couples in the halls and then in the permanent pages of the school yearbook as "Cutest Couple," and hearing about how so-and-so made out with some-other-person over the weekend made me feel like I was a forty-year-old virgin. I didn't want to rush into anything (not that there was anyone to rush into anything with) because everyone else seemed to be, but at the same time, I couldn't help but feel like teen years were the ones everyone spent accomplishing their sexual and romantic firsts: first kiss, first relationship, first time having sex.

It wasn't limited to school either. TV shows and books boasted it too, like the characters on *Degrassi* who were always getting into each other's pants (and don't get me started on those MTV and CW shows). I didn't buy it—they were all clearly a bunch of over-sexualized teens, most of whom were American anyway—and yet, I saw/heard it all around me in real life. So perhaps, in a way, I had been socially conditioned since I was young to expect and find that special someone, or conditioned to be optimistic in the pursuit of finding a mate.

These shows never portrayed the perpetually single. I suppose the lack of plots and arcs wouldn't make for very compelling characters. Even the single-for-a-while eventually encountered love, or a meet-cute would happen upon them and alter their lives irrevocably (like *The Forty-Year-Old Virgin*).

I watched, read, imagined, and waited for my time to come as those around me paired up, one by one. And I waited. And waited.

Because it had to happen to me.

It had to.

I receive an email one afternoon from my Australian pen pal with the subject "no words." In it, there are in fact a great many words. He tells me how he recently downloaded Grindr on his iPhone and has been exchanging messages with someone.

"He's... amazing. We talked on the phone for over half an hour and sent each other some cute texts. This is amazing, Aaron. Nothing like this has happened to me in my life. I've never gone this far with a guy or felt this way. He's good-looking, interesting, and so articulate! He shares just enough about himself to not go too far but he's not boring. He's just... wow." And on and on he goes.

It is then that I am surprised to feel that familiar pit grind itself a few inches deeper in my gut. The same thing happens when Bekki gossips about her evening spent messaging an old friend which ended with the two of them sleeping together.

I wish I had control over how my mind and body react to

good news like this because my friends deserve to be happy, but it appears beyond my power. It is a physiological reflex. Don't get me wrong. Somewhere inside, I am elated for my pen pal and for Bekki and all the others who find someone, but that joy is overwhelmed by a stronger sensation at the same time.

Kavita J. Patel, a blogger and self-proclaimed "love coach," wrote a blog post titled "How to Stop Feeling Jealous of Your Friend's Relationship"[16] that describes "a little feeling tugging at you" upon hearing a friend's good news, such as an engagement. Irish writer Elizabeth Bowen wrote, quite accurately, "Jealousy is no more than feeling alone against smiling enemies." In the exam scenario, when you observe others going up to the front with their finished papers, it is only natural you might be a bit jealous. They have finished and now they get to go out and relax with their friends. Whether they have passed or failed is wholly irrelevant; watching them self-assuredly march up to the front is enough to stir up envy. It makes you feel as if the test is supposed to be simple, which means you're doing something wrong and you need to fix it and hurry the hell up, for god's sake.

On the off-chance things do turn out in my favour, I do a double-take. When I first messaged a guy from a Craigslist ad, I thought for sure he would stop replying as soon as I shared my picture. It always happened like that—especially because he was white, tall, and younger (in general, younger white guys don't seem to be into Asian guys, but that's a whole oth-

16 Kavita J. Patel, "How to stop feeling jealous of your friend's relationship," May 31, 2004, *Kavita J Patel,* https://kavitajpatel.com/blog/2014/05/31/the-real-reason-youre-jealous-of-her-wedding.

er thing). So I was astounded when he asked if I wanted to meet sometime. *Something's wrong,* I thought. *Didn't he get my pic? Why is he still messaging me? Whatever. When we meet, he'll definitely not want to see me again.*

But he did. We met again and cuddled for a bit. When he told me he liked me, I was speechless, utterly bewildered. Every time we were together, I kept wondering the same thing: *Why hasn't he left me yet?* At the end of the summer, he told me he had decided to go back to Germany, where he was from, to study at university. The last time I saw him before he departed, as he broke the news, he teared up. I recall it being peculiar that someone was crying over not being able to see me anymore—peculiar because boys were not supposed to cry over me when they left. I believed they did it coldly, indifferently. I was simply a loose end that required tying up before moving on.

I suppose I did anticipate him going off with somebody else (such as one of the other hotter guys who I imagined must have replied to his ad). Perhaps I have acquired a type of learned helplessness when dating, a paradox of hope and cynicism: things with a potential lover could possibly lead somewhere but in all likelihood, he will ultimately leave me in the dust.

Then there were the other occasions, when the fangs sank in more deeply. Daniel, a handsome guy from Montreal, let me know he wasn't looking for a relationship, only friends. Perhaps naively, I thought I might be able to change his mind after we went on a date; once he saw how awesome I was, he would at least reconsider. We had a pleasant outing, watching

Kiki's Delivery Service at the Cinematheque; sharing a slice of cheesecake on the outdoor patio of Trees Organic Coffee; and having casual, witty, natural conversation.

I should have known we were not going to be together, or maybe I simply refused to believe it. Either way, I couldn't deny it any longer when he texted me one day, *I suppose I must tell you I'm currently living with a former and now current boyfriend. It was quite unexpected. Regardless I felt that was important to say.*

Unexpected.

The way it was phrased, it was as if Daniel woke up one day and his boyfriend showed up on his doorstep like a package. The burn seared more this time because not only had he not been looking for anything, but that it seemed so effortless to fall into a relationship.

I was lagging behind those who weren't trying, akin to other students in the class acing the exam when they could not have cared less about the course (like those who take first-year Creative Writing classes simply for the GPA boost). Or like teammates on the hockey team who didn't train as intensely getting drafted into the NHL, or aspiring mothers becoming pregnant on their first attempt. As we watch others get the one thing we want, the anguish becomes easy to name: defeat.

It may be common to impel yourself to be happy for another person's fortune, but it is discomforting. Besides jealousy, rejection is the other most obvious diagnosis. I have been rejected so many times, it is actually funny (Really. If I had the stats, we would all be laughing). Then again, I have tried so much that it is only logical to have been rejected on countless occasions as well. Men telling me they are dating someone else is a type of rejection, albeit indirectly (it reminds me of uninterested straight girls who tell guys that they already have boyfriends as a gentle way to let them down).

I met John at a sex club—where I wasn't having sex like you're probably thinking (for those wondering what a sex club is like, this one consisted of several rooms including a small dance floor, a backroom with some sex equipment like a sling, a row of stalls, some gloryholes, and a "slurp ramp." Don't ask me about the slurp ramp). Immediately, we hit it off. We spent an hour hanging out by the bar chatting, while half-naked guys awkwardly cruised each other nearby. It was so refreshing to meet another gay guy who didn't mind talking and getting to know each other (and in a sex club, of all places). After that night, we kept in touch, texting each other every once in a while.

When I asked John one night if he wanted to hang out, he told me he was going on a date. Instances such as this makes me feel as if guys don't consider me as anything more than a friend or friend-with-benefits for whatever reason, or that I am not boyfriend material in their eyes. The latter, if it is the case, makes me sad. If only I could make them see.

With Owen, I hadn't even met him in person yet, and he chose to dedicate his time to someone else. Admittedly, I had been repeatedly vague about when to finally meet him, partly because of my busy school and work schedule, as well as all the other things happening in my life. Is this trapdoor-plummet in my stomach regret of things I could have done, or things I did wrong, of a missed opportunity? After all, because I have been single for most of my life and because I seldom go on dates, those I do go out with I deem to be special or different in some way, more interesting than the plethora of basic gays out there. A certain attachment, of connection, forms, and if there is chemistry, even more so. When they desert me for someone else, that severing slams the door on anything I may have hoped would develop between us, leaving me to ruminate over what I should have done or did wrong. It's like I have failed.

Failure.

It is there, a thorn in a garden of weeds, underneath the jealousy, sadness, and hurt. Failure possesses power once importance has been placed on it; some of the other students taking the same exam wouldn't feel bad if they didn't care about passing or not. They could have drawn penises and written "FUCK THIS SHIT" on their papers.

I have a friend who was thinking about going on exchange to Germany, much to her boyfriend's chagrin. She told me that if she went, she wouldn't attempt a long-distance relationship.

"I could meet someone in Germany or he could meet someone else here, so what would be the point? He told me he doesn't want to date anyone else though," she said with a laugh. "When I return, if we're both still single and depending on what else is going on in our lives, we might get back together." The way she talked about leaving him so nonchalantly, like he was a sweater she could leave at home and do without on her travels made me question, *How are you able to let go of him like that after being together for years? Doesn't he mean anything to you?* Although I understand her perspective, I personally would have tried my best to make things work if I were in a relationship with someone I loved before terminating it so quickly.

I believe I value love more than the average person. I was born to love, yes, but I also try harder than anyone else I know. So when the hockey player breaks his leg and is out for the season, and the woman has a false positive upon taking a pregnancy test, and I fail in love, it hurts more than for the average person. The hockey player is more devastated than the teammate who enjoys playing recreationally. The woman is more upset than the other who became pregnant on her first attempt to start a family. After all the time and effort, all the training, learning, and practice, after making it a priority in life—to watch others move ahead, seemingly so effortlessly, that is why I feel like I have been left in the dust.

I have not simply failed in love. I have failed my purpose.

The average person, it seems, isn't torn apart when a date goes off with someone else. They don't go dissecting their emotions in personal essays or silently crying themselves to sleep. When it comes to dating, they consider it part of the game. Everyone is out there, all searching; it is inevitable that some find their partners before others. You win some, you lose some. Then you move on to the next.

An online article by blogger Thea Easterby, "Does It Feel

Like Everyone is Moving Forward – Except You?"[17] offers those feeling left behind some useful advice, like "You need to be patient" and "Run your own race." The author also suggests to "accept you may be on a different path," which immediately makes me narrow my eyes in suspicion. She prefaces this point by stating that some of us might not like this piece of advice, which probably means I won't like it.

To help illustrate her point, she gives an example of how you might want to walk down the aisle like all of your friends, "but not everyone has children, not everyone meets their soul mate. The point is to realize that going down another path is okay. You simply might be destined for other amazing, fabulous things in life. Life doesn't (and probably shouldn't) be about everyone following a set life template. After all, what we want in life is not a one-size-fits-all proposition."

In this proposed reality, I am supposed to be content being single, and although this is entirely possible, I cannot for the life of me imagine it. I picture myself having coffee with friends and chatting about our love lives. After complaining about how they have to passive-aggressively tell their husbands to take out the compost bin when it is full, they ask how mine is, to which I reply with a confident smile, "No, there's no one. But I'm perfectly fine." It seems so bizarre, so unlike me, like some alternate-universe version of myself.

When I bemoan my online dating woes to a friend, he assures me that his friend's mother is unabashedly doing the same thing. People of all ages are looking for love, he insists.

17 Thea Easterby, "Does It Feel Like Everyone is Moving Forward – Except You?" *Write Change Grow,* May 2011, https://www.writechangegrow.com/2011/05/does-it-feel-like-everyone-is-moving-forward-except-you.

But instead of comforting me, his advice has the opposite effect; the thought of being fifty or sixty and still searching for someone scares me not only because I will be older (which is difficult to imagine in itself; for many years, I had an inexplicable feeling that I wasn't going to live past thirty), but after years and years of trying as hard as I am now, it will all have led to nothing. Somewhere along the way, I may have had a relationship or two, but for whatever reason, they didn't pan out. The image I conjure as the fifty-year-old me wears a perpetually sad face, sunken eyes that dejectedly scan profiles of younger men who, upon all these years of trying, still don't respond to me.

The prospect of being on another path—one where I am alone and watching others move forward—can't be my future, can it? Obviously, it is nowhere near the worst thing that could happen to me (working a soul-sucking, unfulfilling desk job would be worse), but nonetheless, I reject this possibility. I want to tell myself it is not my destiny. At the same time, things don't exactly seem too promising these days.

When I tell my best friend Chelsea about being born to love, she is contemplative for a minute. "Well, it's difficult because your happiness, your goal, depends on someone else." It's not like I can force someone to let me love them (although for the right price, I am sure someone would at least attempt to do it. Or fake it). Like the would-be mother, we both depend on someone else, and this factor is what makes our goals harder to achieve than others'.

Perhaps, as Easterby suggests, I should accept that I may end up alone. I think of those passionate, enthusiastic contestants on *American Idol,* their smiles beaming through the television screen before they enter the fateful room of judges, the hopefuls who confess they have been singing since they came into this world and have always known in their hearts without a doubt it is their calling. And then the aftermath, when Simon Cowell tells them they will never in a million years make it and that they should quit, they sob outside in the hallways. How many of them listen to his advice and stop singing forever? How many give up what they must feel is their purpose in life?

When I delete my profile on Plenty of Fish, one that I created when I was nineteen, it urges me to reconsider: "64% of users leaving Plenty of Fish have found someone here. You're so close to finding that someone special! Don't give up now!" There they are, appealing to my conditioned optimism by trying to persuade me with more optimism. The implication is that I, too, can be part of the majority that encounters love and that my romantic plot, like in the narratives I read and watched, will happen shortly with a few clicks and keystrokes. Because the alternative—is simply unfathomable.

The reality is that it does not always work out for everyone. We can't all be in the sixty-four percent. Maybe my place is with the other thirty-six.

Maybe the hockey player isn't meant to be a hockey player and becomes an accountant.

Maybe the woman isn't meant to be a mother and ends up fostering kittens.

In the meantime, I am still sitting in that classroom, struggling to complete the exam I may never end up completing while more and more people finish ahead of me. After some time, the only sound I hear is the clock on the wall above me, the hands of which constantly snatch away my life in fragments and reverberate throughout the progressively vacant hall.

Tick, tock. Tick, tock. Tick, tock...

IN THE MOVIES

WHEN my relationship with Samuel, my first boyfriend, ended, the counselor I saw a year later offered me a helpful metaphor. My thoughts and dreams of Sam—of finally sharing a bed together for a night, of opening the door to our house to welcome our friends for Thanksgiving dinner, of kissing him and breathing in his scent again before he smiles up at me—are contained in a box that sits on a shelf in my mind. I notice this box every day, but until things change, I cannot touch or open it. On a cold winter night, I bring the box with me to meet the man inside.

Even in the dark of his old red car, Sam looks the same as the twenty-one-year-old I fell in love with five years ago: his loose, dark hair; the thin, metal-framed glasses resting just below the bridge of his small nose; his lips I would kiss. He's still young and handsome. There is one thing that's different: he's wearing leather driving gloves, and I can't help but think they should belong to a murderer on a crime show. I can almost hear the creak of stretching leather as they close themselves around an unsuspecting victim's throat.

Sam says he will drive around the neighborhood while we talk, and I secretly wish we could just drive far away somewhere and never come back. It would be so easy. Instead, he thanks me for the handwritten letter I sent him last week, and when I don't respond, I can tell he's working up to what he needs to say.

His voice drops lower, cutting right to the point: "Aaron, I'm not comfortable with how things are between us. I know it has been difficult after your last boyfriend, but when you contact me, I feel like you're expecting us to get back together. And if I respond, it's as bad as if I don't. You put me in a very uncomfortable position," he says with a weary sigh.

I don't know what to say to that, so I change the topic: "I know you told me before how you honestly thought your mom would kill you if she found out, but is that really the only reason?"

"No."

"Then what is it? I'm not accusing you, I just want to understand."

He hesitates. "I can't explain it," he manages, a line he's used before. "I can't see myself going down that road." The car halts at a red light.

"It's not who I am," he simply states.

"You're gay. That's a fact. Whether or not you do anything about it is irrelevant. You can deny it, but that's who you are," I refute, struggling to contain the anger in my voice.

"Believe me when I say I've been thinking about this a lot. I've done some growing up these past years. I've been dealing with moral issues. I tried things out, and decided it wasn't right for me." We drive ahead. He signals right to turn down a dim street. Meanwhile, questions ricochet and echo in my head. *Moral issues? Tried it out? Not right for him? Has he slept with other guys? Are those hateful religious beliefs finally getting to him?*

"You told me before I have a choice. Well, this is my choice," he says.

The screaming in my head says he's wrong, but I steady myself. "What are you going to do in a few years when your mom, your friends, and relatives start questioning you about why you're not married? Would you actually be with a woman or someone you don't love? I just... really don't want you to become one of those guys."

Sam huffs. "You might not understand this," he growls slightly, "but to me, it doesn't matter who I love. When I was with my girlfriend, I loved her. We broke up because of irreconcilable differences. Then you and I were together and I loved you. I feel comfortable loving someone—man or woman. It doesn't matter."

When I met him, he told me he was bisexual. I was nineteen then. It didn't seem like a big deal. After we got into a relationship, I asked him about it again. "Yeah, I'm gay," he conceded at the time.

As he continues driving down lonely streets, I attempt reason: "Just because something is easier to do, doesn't mean it's the right or the best thing to do."

"Look, after my girlfriend and I broke up, I was curious about this gay stuff, and I admit I missed loving someone. So I went online and... I didn't expect to go so far with it and to hurt you. I feel guilty for messing things up for you, even now."

I do my best to conceal the tremble in my voice in anticipation of an answer I don't want to hear. "Do you regret what happened between us?"

"No, but I want you to move on and find someone who loves you the way you deserve, who can be the boyfriend I can't be for you."

"But you can! You just won't!"

Sam slows the car and parks half a block away from my house. "What do you want me to do?"

"Well, ideally, come out to—"

"See? That's not what I want! I don't want that." He takes a breath. "It's been, how long since we were together now?"

My voice cracks. "Almost five years."

"I know that it's been difficult for you to get over us, especially since I was your first. I worry about what you're going to do after this, especially how upset you were with your ex. I'm afraid that you'll..."

"Kill myself?" I finish for him.

"I was afraid you'd say that. Please promise me you won't do anything stupid." I see him glance over at me with concern all over his face, but I don't respond.

As I process everything, I swallow, but the stone remains lodged in my throat. "I know you might not understand why I keep hanging on to you. I've let go of the possibility of getting back with my other ex. I genuinely feel like that will never happen. But for whatever reason, I have this idea of you and me in the future, and I know that it's stupid and ridiculous, since we were only together for four months, but I can't help it. I'm sorry."

There's a slow exhale of air from Sam before he says, "I'm tired, Aaron." I glance over at the digital clock. It's past two in the morning. "I'm tired of thinking about all this."

I look out the window. Darkened houses line the street. I imagine couples sleeping together in warm beds, holding each other. Sam's voice brings me back to the present.

"What do we do now?" Sam asks.

"Well, I'm not crying now, but when I've had the chance to think about it, I will be. You'll go back home, get some sleep, and the world will continue on." He says nothing.

"You win."

"This isn't a game," he chokes out.

"You win," I repeat. *You get what you want, I don't.*

Sam starts the ignition and drives up to the middle of the street outside my house. He puts the car in park and lets the engine run, implying I should go, but I don't want to leave it like this. Dangling from the rearview mirror is a chrome decoration: the word "hope." I can't help but chuckle and stroke it with my finger.

"This," I say, "This is what I've been holding onto all these years. I guess there isn't any left anymore." Silence. He doesn't even glance over.

I tell him the last thing I could possibly say that might change his mind, or at the very least, will leave him with something to think about.

"I will always love you, you know."

When I look over at him, he's staring straight ahead. Suddenly, I'm hit with the thought of what a character in a film would do in this scene, and I fight the urge to touch his hand or give him a kiss on the cheek, to show him that it's not wrong to be with me. Instead, I climb out of his car and step alone into the frozen night. I force myself not to turn around as I walk back up to my house. Instead of entering through the front door, I head around back. Out of sight, I lean against the rough bumps of the stucco wall of the house and shut my eyes tightly. I want to cry, but my eyes refuse—for now. In the distance, I hear the engine of his car fade away down the road.

The next day, Chelsea tells me that I did all I could. Perhaps being with someone he might not truly love will compound over time and get to him eventually, she suggests. But I am not convinced; I picture him smiling with his girlfriend or wife, with his children, taking family photos for the ages while day after day, he ignores the closet door of his true identity, boarded and cemented up years ago like an abandoned store.

When we were together, I always knew it was right. When I kissed you, it felt right. I know you knew it too, I write to Sam in a final email a couple days later.

***

I have this little picture of my life several years in the future. It goes something like this:

INT. HOUSE — KITCHEN — DAY

In a quiet kitchen room illuminated by warm daylight, a MAN sits at the table, slowly fixing himself some toast and juice. As he sits down to eat, the doorbell RINGS.

The Man gets up and walks to the door. His face doesn't change as he looks through the window at the visitor. After a beat, he opens the door.

Another MAN stands there, a small, worn leather suitcase

next to him on the welcome mat. The two men stare at each other for a few seconds. Then, the first Man smiles, opens the door wider and gestures to the visitor to enter.

The second Man picks up his suitcase and steps inside. The door closes behind him.

FADE OUT.

And then I remember. There is no box of dreams anymore.

This is only in the movies.

Underworld

I don't know why I'm here.

Before I left home, I told myself it was because I didn't want to listen to my mom's grating voice anymore while she yelled on the phone. On the SkyTrain, I convinced myself that my soul aches, that after years of searching and countless failed attempts at dating, this is the final place where I have to be able to find the cure to my hurt—a fellow soul to connect with and relate to. And as I walked over, I admitted that I might simply be horny and wanting to fool around with other guys, something I didn't get a chance to do when I visited with a friend last week. What I do know, as I stand before the grand, weathered wooden doors, ones that look like a gate to another realm, is that it's probably a bad idea to enter—but it feels too late to turn back. It could be that I've come all this way and don't want to leave for nothing, but the doors somehow suck me in, as if I've strayed too close to its gravitational field and now I'm falling in, crashing. *I should go,* I think as I grasp the handle and pull the door open, *yet I can't.*

Inside the dim lobby is a window with a space between it and the counter below to pass money and cards through; it reminds me of a movie theatre's box office. I make out the muffled bass beats of a dance track beyond the metal door next to the window; It sounds vacuous, void of feeling, and I don't understand why they play music like that here. Then again, I can't imagine what it would be like to have good music like Sarah McLachlan or Debussy blaring on the speakers overhead while I'm sucking off a stranger.

"Could I just get a locker, please?" I ask the guy standing behind the spotless glass. He has dark stubble and wears a friendly smile, his hair neatly combed and slick with gel. The patches on his pressed grey uniform make him look like an auto mechanic. One stitched on the left of his shirt reads "Freddy."

"Sure. Do you have a membership?"

Clumsily, I retrieve the student membership card I signed up for last week. Freddy punches in the info and charges me the fee for the locker. Behind me, the doors open and traffic noise spills in. I don't turn around to see who it is; I'm too afraid to meet their eyes, for them to see me as I see them— yet another sleazy gay guy looking for an anonymous fuck. I know that's not me.

"Come on in." There's a buzz and a mechanical switch as the door unlocks. I funnel through to the other side as if on a river. Three older men, two completely naked and one with a towel, swivel their three heads at me simultaneously and stare. I look away. Many younger Asian guys are into older white men, but that has never been the case for me. I have always been interested in men around my age or younger; race has never been a factor for me. Combined with years of being fetishized and objectified by older, bigger, white men, they make me feel like prey in their eyes, in their big, groping hands. About to be devoured whole.

"Your locker number is 434," Freddy informs me, placing a

key on a folded, dryer-warm towel on the counter. In Chinese culture, the number four is a bad-luck number: a homophone for "death." I try not to think about how my mom would immediately demand another locker—or her disgust if she saw me here at all.

In the locker area, I strip and cover myself with the towel like everyone else. *Glasses on or off?* I debate internally. People seem to think glasses are unattractive (god knows some of the shallowest people I've ever met are gay men), but I decide to leave them on. I know how gloomy it is around.

Okay, well, I'm here. But I can still have a good night. I have the power to do that, to say no if I need to. We'll just take it easy, relax a bit, and see where things go. Let's start with the steam room. Pep talk over, after locking up my clothes, I tread on the wet brown tiles of the shower area, where a few men are bathing comfortably as if they shower next to other nude men all the time. A burst of hot vapour hits me when I open the steam-room door.

It's quiet. Although the steam effectively renders my glasses useless, I make out the outlines of others nearby. They look like ghosts; the steam makes them seem translucent. I sit down and imagine what it would be like if the steam weren't there, if it were just a room full of mostly naked men sitting around in silence.

No one touches each other. No one says anything. We sit there, waiting for something to happen, praying the next guy coming in brings some action with him. But nothing happens. Which is fine for me because I'm satisfied relaxing and sweating in the steam. This night might not be so bad after all.

After a little while, I need to breathe, so I take a quick shower and decide to go for a stroll around the main floor. Across from the showers are steps leading up to a bubbling hot tub, where the heads and shoulders of three people seem to float above the water motionless. In the faded light, the water appears dirty, tinged brown. Just outside one of the two doors to the joined shower/Jacuzzi space is a short row of private rooms. I suspect these rooms must be the most expensive, ones with the largest, comfiest beds and other perks. I haven't seen anyone enter or exit these doors. I wonder if I'll ever be invited into one.

There are a couple guys in the small gym area working out. One of them is heaving a barbell naked. Light fur covers his chest and legs—a muscular cub, if I had to choose a label. Based on previous interactions with the same kind of guy, I'm willing to bet my life that I'm not his type, so I move on, trying to ignore feeling disappointed. Close by, there's the clanging of lockers, unzipping of zippers, unbuckling of belts before they knock on benches, shoes scuffing the floor as they're kicked off. I poke my head in to see the new arrivals, feeling a thrill run through me like a lit fuse. When I realize what I'm doing—being a creepy voyeur, like the other men—I have to leave.

A few paces away, concealed by a curtain, is what resembles a black, glory hole-type structure that I don't go near—it looks sketchy. Some men lounge in leather seats, ogling those who walk by. Next to the stairs, two wooden picnic tables are opposite a large, high-definition flatscreen TV, but no one is watching. Freddy and his co-workers are laughing and joking amongst themselves and other half-covered men nearby. A stout, hairy man with a belly peruses the options of anal douches and hoses in a vending machine. Receding hairlines and wrinkles suggest the average age in here is maybe mid-forties. Everything feels so bizarre, like an alternate dimension that operates on its own rules, its own logic. Should I relate to all this because I'm gay? But there's nothing here I can identify with, aside from the commonality of sex with men. It all makes me doubt again the reason for my presence.

There's not much else I feel I can do, or at least no one I want to do it with, so I return to the steam room—to the sound of moaning. A larger man is sitting down, his towel splayed open below him on the bench. On his knees in front is a smaller guy. I take a seat across from them and watch, getting turned on. After a few moments, the older man abruptly leans over and whispers some muffled words to his servicer, grabs his towel, and exits. I expect the younger guy to follow him, but he only stands up and watches the glass door close. It takes him a few seconds to notice me.

He steps over and, without hesitation, touches my chest, my back, down to my crotch. The sweat on his fingers makes them feel slimy as he slides his palm all over my skin. It's not really what I want, but it's not completely awful either. Situations like this don't happen to me, and not knowing what to do, I sit there and caress his damp skin a bit. When our eyes meet, I see he's young, perhaps younger than my twenty-five years. Suddenly, I can't help but think of him as someone's child. *You shouldn't be here,* I tell him telepathically.

Instead, he kneels again and resumes where he left off.

It feels fine—it's clear he knows what he's doing—yet there seems to be something missing.

I feel him on me, but nothing else. No magical spark, no passion. An empty intimate act. I find myself averting my eyes from him—towards the benches across, the ceiling melting and dripping water, anything. My soul cries out for something else, but my pulse drowns it out by drumming in my ears. I swallow hard. It takes me minutes as the question struggles and finally clobbers its way out of my mouth.

"When was the last time you were tested?" It feels strange and almost taboo to break the silence, like I've violated a law. My voice sounds dubbed over by someone else.

"Last month. You?"

"Oh, okay. Me too."

I nod out of nervousness, a habit, and he mistakes it as his cue to carry on. The nothingness returns. *You don't have to do this. Can we just talk for a bit instead?* But the words are too strong, too big to force out. So I endure him as well as the discomfort. After a while, he stands up, presenting me with his hard dick.

"Suck it," he whispers. I take his cock—slippery from sweat, steam, and pre-cum—and tug on it, trying to buy myself some time while I get acquainted with it. He must sense my hesitation because he adds, "Just a little. Please."

It would be kind of rude to say no, since he did the same for me. At the same time, maybe it's how moist it is, but his dick isn't very appealing. *Just a little*, I think, before I take him in my mouth. I battle the urge to retch.

While this goes on, more and more guys enter the room

and loiter. Out of the corner of my eye, I see them hovering; some leer, while others touch themselves as they watch this impromptu porno I didn't mean to star in, which only intensifies my emptiness and makes me feel dirty. He must sense them too because he rises, leans over, and whispers into my ear.

"Let's get out of here."

With that, he takes my hand and leads me out of the steam; I'm aware of the heads and eyes trailing us as we vacate the room, relieved to be rid of the audience. We bypass the showers and approach the glory-hole booth. When he goes in, I hesitate. I have zero interest in getting off in a glory hole. And what would be the point? I've already seen what he looks like.

But as I draw back the curtain, I'm surprised to see ascending stairs. Following him up the creaky, narrow, wooden staircase, we reach an enclosed area with a raised platform. Even with my glasses on, everything, including our white towels, is shades of black. He pulls me to him and forces his tongue into my mouth. As a reflex, my tongue retreats inside my mouth, and I wonder if he can tell I don't really want to kiss him. If he knows, he ignores it. When we break, again, he kneels. This is supposed to be enjoyable, so why am I not enjoying it? I should try. I close my eyes and tell myself that it's good, it's good.

Nearby, the wooden stairs groan. A shadowed head peers out from behind the wall and watches us. He shuffles over, touching himself, his hard dick swinging in front of the young guy on his knees, who gobbles it up as well. This man appears to be older and instinctively, I want to shrink away from him.

His tongue glides across my throat. I twist my neck away from his slobbering mouth, hoping he will receive the signal to not move higher. When he touches my skin, I flinch so hard I nearly jump: his hands are so smooth, it's as if there are no lines or creases in them, like he's rubbing me with heated mittens. Like he isn't human.

"I want you to fuck me." The younger guy is on his feet again, his breath on my ear causing an involuntary shudder throughout my body. Possible answers spin around like a game-show wheel: *I don't; Can we keep doing this instead?; How about this guy fucks you instead?; Are you sure you don't want us to get to know each other a bit first?* After a few seconds, I manage to choke out the most appropriate response I can think of. "Let's go find a condom."

He withdraws and yanks his towel off the platform. For a moment, it seems like things are off. Then, he leans in again and replies, "I'll go get one. Wait here for me." He wanders down the rickety stairway.

I hope the man with velvet hands will leave too, but instead he manoeuvres himself behind me; while he handles me and grinds his dick against my ass, growling "Oh yeahhh," I am a cadaver, wide-eyed, paralyzed, and mute. I can't help but think back to a poster above the urinals at university, educating students about consent with a list of points. One of them was that "consent is a freely given and enthusiastic yes!" *So this is what it must feel like to be sexually assaulted. Should I be traumatized? I feel... nothing.*

Eventually, he must get bored of me stiffly standing there

and surrenders. Alone in the silence, I sigh. For the first time since I've arrived, I feel comfortable and calm in the solitude, and I spend these moments collecting myself. That was a pretty awful experience, but this young guy doesn't seem half bad, even if I'm not completely into what he's doing. Maybe if I keep doing things with him, the nothingness will transform into somethingness. Yes, that must happen.

As I wait for him to return, a few others stumble into my hideaway. One has an African accent and purrs, "Come with me. I have a room," to which I announce, with confidence for once, "I'm waiting for someone."

To kill time, I examine my surroundings. I notice a hole under the platform, large enough to fit my face; the hues inside are lighter than the dark where I am, indicative of a different room. It turns out to be a massive, dark play space of sorts, in which there are nooks and corners in jagged shapes and no clear path through. Shadows occasionally drift in and out, almost floating by. They slow as they approach other dark shapes, but there is never any contact. They come in alone, they leave alone.

It takes about ten minutes of pacing in the dark before I spot a glimmer of something on top of the black-painted platform.

A condom. Still sealed in the packaging.

Did he see it? Surely, condoms aren't that hard to obtain here; the front desk probably has tons, and it's only down the hall. Maybe he was offended I wanted to use a condom and instead found somebody else. In any case, he should be back by now.

With another sigh, I gather my towel and descend. I don't find him on the main level, which means either he's left or he is downstairs.

The bottom floor is a web of two main corridors, with shorter paths abruptly jutting out from them at sharp angles. I think back to my first time and the disorientation I experienced, like being in a labyrinth. Private rooms line these hallways, lit in a red, hellish haze. Past that is a completely pitch-black area. Needless to say, I'm not particularly excited to wander down there again. *At least you know your way around this time,* I assure myself with every cautious step down the vinyl, non-slip stairs.

The first thing I see is a mirror and sink area. I turn away from the mirror. Another out-of-place dance song blasts on the speakers above as I join other non-dancing men shuffling around barefoot on the carpeted floor, doing my best to blend in. Eyes meet other eyes, hands find skin occasionally. Men pose by the doors of their rooms, trying to balance interest and casualness, taking in everyone who strolls by in an attempt to lure others into their caves. A few doors I pass are open: inside, some men are un-toweled and masturbating; others have blue faces, illuminated by a hanging television in the corner. Others are simply lying there with their asses or legs up in the air, poised and ready to be taken. Maybe it's from having watched all sorts of gay porn for years or simply that I'm not shocked easily, but none of what I see fazes me. Some of it is a little unexpected, but this is gay life, after all. And for tonight, I am a visitor.

I spy the young guy after a lap around the maze and call

out from behind. He turns and barely glances at me as we briefly make eye contact. Then he turns back and continues down the hall in the opposite direction. I stand there, dumbfounded and hurt, and not knowing what else to do, I begin walking too. Why make a big deal out of something—someone—as trivial as a hookup? Guys fuck and leave. That's the way they do things. They'd laugh at me for being emotional, for being a girl. I should at least pretend it meant nothing.

In one room, a young, handsome man lies on the bed, facing the door. After passing by at least four times, I vow to go in and say hi, chat with him a bit. He looks like he wants to talk to someone.

When I find his room again, I linger by the doorway. Our eyes lock, and I watch him jerk off for a few seconds. Taking this as a good sign, I cautiously take a step inside.

"No, sorry," he blurts. Immediately, I withdraw.

"Oh. No problem." I add a laugh so he'll think it's just a casual misunderstanding, all in good fun, before I depart.

Another guy is sitting on a bench against a wall, watching men in suits having sex on TV. I wonder if he's resigned and jaded like me when it comes to talking with guys. Again, I have to talk myself up before taking a seat next to him. He doesn't look over. When I say hi, he responds with silence, seemingly rapt, transfixed by what will happen next in the film. I sit there for a few seconds, letting the rejection sting and sink in like a needle in my arm before getting up.

The few men whom I actually want to do something with look right past me as we pass each other in the hallways. There is one standing in a corner whom I stroll by several times. I want to go up to him, but the last encounters have made me nervous about getting rebuffed again. After all, this guy is good-looking and white, and I've been rejected by good-looking white guys ever since I started dating. Every time I walk past the guy in the corner, I long for him to notice me, but his eyes are always elsewhere, looking through my chest, past my head. Finally, he's simply gone. It shouldn't make sense to feel disappointment about a stranger. And yet in my head, it's another opportunity out the window, hope dissolved.

I assume he's in the other part of the floor, past the violet-tinted urinals and showers, in the black area. There, no one sees one another as they either watch or take turns servicing a row of men lined up against metal prison bars, or stuff themselves inside confined, tight stalls. Everyone is the same: faceless silhouettes. Last time, I was puzzled by how everyone was able to be turned on by someone they couldn't see; I suppose it could be thrilling, though.

The sound of moaning emanates even before I've entered. I inch past a beefy guy with big pecs positioned just outside the prison, observing what appears to be a shapeless black monster of disproportionate appendages writhing and pleasuring itself. Our skin grazes each other's, and instead of continuing on, I park myself a couple feet away from him. Since it's too dark to see anything happening near the prison bars, I turn my attention to him by tentatively reaching out and touching his chest. His shorter height and smooth skin are like those of a younger jock-type guy, and when he touches me back, a wave of excitement travels outwards from his hand. *Someone I like seems to like me too!* I can't see his face, but it seems only logical a hot body matches a hot guy.

We feel each other up for a while before he walks towards the exit. I take the hint to follow him as we breach incandescent light once again and my vision returns. His chest and body are exactly what I felt: muscular, taut. But when I look further up, there are lines on his face; his eyes seem weathered. He looks at least forty. The possibility that he might be twice my age is a thought I try not to dwell on. I almost wish we had stayed cloaked in the dark. I begin coming up with polite excuses to leave when he asks, "Do you want to go back to my room?"

"Uh, sure," I lie for some reason.

As he fumbles to open the door to his room in the faint light, I notice everyone's gazes on us. I want to tell them, *No, we're not hooking up! I don't even find him that attractive. And I don't know why I'm going in with him!* Once inside, he lies down on the small cot that almost fills the entire cramped room and gestures for me to join him. Suddenly aware of the situation—he wants to have sex with me and I don't want to, but I'm now locked in a room with him—I merely sit on my heels next to him, unmoving, like I've been turned to stone.

"You're really cute. Sexy," he tells me. I thank him and reply that I'm nervous.

"You didn't seem nervous in there, touching me and licking my chest," he says with a chuckle. I don't chuckle back. *I thought you were someone else*, I want to say. Instead, I ask for the time. He turns on the television and flips through multiple channels, all porn. Apparently, there isn't anything else besides that.

"I'd say probably around one?"

I nod. "I don't live downtown, so I have to make sure I can still get home."

"I see. It's good to make sure you can get home." I don't know what to say, so I nod again.

"You're very sexy," he repeats, his smile stretching into a Cheshire cat's grin.

A few moments pass. "I, um, I think I should go. I'm sorry."

He gets up from the bed. "No, no, it's fine." I'm glad he doesn't make a big deal of it or call me out as leading him on or anything. We put our respective towels around us again, and he opens the door. I step out and turn around, about to wish him goodbye, only to find his back to me as he returns to the shadow-prison.

As I walk away, I think about the men who freely touched my skin, the same skin I declared years ago I would only allow those who meant something to me to touch, and I shiver. I glance down at my own skin, expecting to see the claw marks of strangers' fingers, strangers I could barely even see. I wonder again why I'm here in the middle of the night, how I came to this moment, and I know I need to go. I don't belong here.

My pace quickens as I navigate the tangled passages, trying to find my way out of the labyrinth. When I glance up at the men, their eyes are dark holes, their faces blank and sagging, living *Scream* paintings. *I'm not like them, I'm not like them,* I repeat to myself as I find the stairs and take them two at a time.

Back on the main level, I finally notice the hypnotic, minimalist music. It has a repetitive beat—sa-*la-ciousss* … *sa-la-*

ciousss ... evidently the only lyric to the song. The singer coos the words like a siren, his voice practically dripping with sex and sweat as he alternates between first major, then minor chords in the one word—a musical descent into hell. Everything—including now the music—seems to be urging me to stay, which only exacerbates my need to flee and the disgust I have for myself.

I want to leave, but my dick doesn't unless I finish it off. Since I don't have a private room and don't know where else to get off, I opt for the showers, ignoring the openness. There's only one other person here and he doesn't even so much as glance over, which makes it all the easier. I hover in front of the motion sensor, recoiling at the sudden burn and the pressurized spray. Near the ceiling are six television screens playing six different porn films of men having hot, passionate sex. Nothing I've seen tonight resembled any of them. Maybe nothing ever will for me.

I look back down to the men adjacent to the steam room door as they ogle one another with lust. They all seem so confident, like they know what they're doing, and yet now all they seem like are lost, desperate souls limping around, entering doors as if trying to find the correct one that will lead them to an afterlife.

And I start to question if I'm destined to become one of these men years from now—a straggling soul, lonely and moaning for consolation, for connection. I see myself wandering these cursed hallways, a now-permanent pocket of a hole in my chest, my face worn and tired like those around me. *To think I ever wanted to leave,* I might think, as I let an older man fondle me in the black.

No, there's no way that could happen. You still have a soul, and you can still save it. But before I can finish the thought, the shower suddenly shuts off, as if it sensed there wasn't a soul there at all.

Minefield

Twenty-nine years I've wandered around,
there's no beauty here,
no emerald town
– "On the Ocean" by Guster

NOBODY moves. So I do.

Then again, Monday mornings on the #43 bus—well, any bus in Vancouver, really—are the same: people who prefer to stand at the front of the bus or adamantly station themselves in the vicinity of the rear doors as if their lives depend on it. Either way, both effectively block passengers from getting on as well as test my suppressed murderous impulses.

From what I observe, the seats today are already filled, mostly by sleepy university students nodding off or still cramming from last night with notebooks in their laps, and young people and working adults alike consciously ignorant of the world around them by either saturating their ears with music or eliminating all peripheral vision to tunnel in on Instagram photos on their phones.

I roll my eyes at the familiar sight. I excuse myself to the throng of standees, and the crowd reluctantly parts somewhat as I journey to the back of the bus. There are a couple people standing in the tail end, flanked by two full rows of seated passengers facing each other. Just as I edge myself past the usual few crowding the back doors and take a step up to the back, I see him.

His head is lowered, gazing down at a textbook. He is wearing a dark leather jacket I have never seen him wear, headphones I have never seen him use. Suddenly, I picture someone giving them to him as a birthday or Christmas gift—the special occasions he has now spent. His life without me.

I carefully retreat a few inches and try to contain the rising in my blood while trying to make as small a scene as possible, so I turn my back to him to face the window opposite. If I return to the front, he might notice me (since people don't usually move up the bus). But at the same time, I sense my heart scaling itself up my throat, my heartbeat accelerating, and my breathing becoming shallower and shallower. I close my eyes but it is no use: I still sense him there, accompanied by a dread creeping up my body.

This familiar feeling of an anxiety attack.

I know I could stand here for the rest of the ride and endure it, but when it comes to fight or flight, I will always take the first plane out. At Cambie Street, with more than halfway still to go to get to university, I practically launch myself out of the bus doors once they open. Somehow, I manage to speed-walk down the block and nearly collapse on the edge of a large planter, where I try to regain control of my breathing. The bus idles at the curb metres away, and I will it to go and leave me alone. But it remains there longer than usual, for seemingly minutes. I wonder if he can see me through the back window now, puzzled at why I'm just sitting here.

After what seems like eons, the bus finally pulls away; calm begins to return. I retrieve my phone from my jacket pocket and find Chelsea's number.

Saw G. on the bus and had to get off because I couldn't handle it. I want to leave this city. I can't handle it anymore.

The aquarium.
Stanley Park.
Giant bus ads for the aquarium.
Burnaby.
UBC and Langara College.
Main Street/Science World Station.
A bench on Davie Street.

Where G. works and where we spent a night sleeping beside a starfish tank.

Where G. and I broke up and where the aquarium is located.

Giant mobile reminders of the past.

Where G. lives.

Where we both went to school.

Where I met G. on the day he told me he was seeing someone.

Where I had my first anxiety attack after he told me.

These sites have become forbidden zones, mines that trigger an onslaught of negative emotions—mostly overwhelming, debilitating sadness—if I stray too close. Usually, I experience a high degree of anxiety; for example, after the bus incident, I was convinced G. could be anywhere at UBC at any time. On various occasions, I mistook other students for him and ended up having minor anxiety attacks. My stress levels spiked whenever I walked around campus. Only in my Creative Writing classes, spaces I knew he would never be in, was I able to relax somewhat. The city I grew up in, the one I used to love, gradually disappeared beneath these invisible explosives, one by one. Vancouver became a minefield.

I was self-aware enough to recognize that certain places affected my mental health, but I had no idea how to cure it. I felt powerless, at the mercy of my own memories and mind. The only thing I could do was to try and avoid the mines, even when they inconvenienced me. After glimpsing G. waiting at the bus stop outside Langara College and then, months later, on the bus going to UBC, I opted for alternate routes to get to and from school, like the slower #41 bus. Every time I boarded, I frantically scanned every face in wide-eyed panic and terror; only when every passenger had been cross-checked and the coast was clear was I able to take a seat without anxiety completely consuming and paralyzing me. On campus, I avoided the biology labs and buildings—even streets—where he might be. Once, upon spotting someone who resembled G. in the Student Union Building, I gasped, darted behind a bulletin board, and as I fought to control my breathing, nervously peeked out from behind it to confirm whether it was him. Fortunately, it was a case of mistaken identity. I sighed heavily with relief, only to nearly crumple to the floor in a heap of tears. Whenever a bus passed by with a giant advertisement of the aquarium on its side, I had to turn away and shut my eyes. Stanley Park and the aquarium were both places

I vowed I would never return to (and as of eight years later, I have yet to revisit either). I couldn't even refer to him by his full name because simply saying or writing it seemed to cause pain, as if his name contained too much weight (and still does, as you can see).

During the winter, I had a seasonal job working the outdoor kiosk at Van Dusen Garden's Festival of Lights, where I made and served food. The garden was also the site of positive emotional significance: on a small bench up on an isolated little hill, as we had sat surrounded by brilliant, multicoloured lights (and also obnoxious, blaring Christmas tunes), G. and I had traded "I love you"s for the first time after dating for a few months. When our relationship ended, it was difficult to work there without ruminating on a ceaseless cycle, especially when business was slow. People always said work was a good distraction for breakups, and I wholeheartedly plunged myself into it, hoping it would sedate and transport me away someplace, anyplace—but to no avail. He was always on the front and back of my mind, the pain and depression clouding over everything I did—regardless whether I was stirring an oversized wok full of popcorn kernels or dispensing hot chocolate. I elected to work there the year after our breakup, but still found myself trying desperately to tune out the cheery Christmas carols and averting my eyes from the shining lights. There didn't seem to be a point in returning if it was only going to cause anguish, and I told the manager I wouldn't be returning after that, claiming a needed rest after a hectic semester at school.

I went as far as to cut myself off from certain people.

Christine was a mutual friend of mine and G.'s who offered comfort and an ear if I ever needed someone to confide in. But as she and I sat inside Breka Bakery on Fraser Street, both of us nursing hot beverages and delectable, sugary pastries, I couldn't help but be reminded of G. since I had met Christine through him. I didn't want to have negative feelings for her— she obviously had not done anything wrong, not to mention she was a good friend—but when she texted to check up on me, I couldn't get past my melancholy and bitterness. I regret that we eventually lost touch.

As it might already be evident, G. left the most mines across the city, but there were others who created minor quakes following their departures. When my grandpa was in the hospital, my mom drove me and my grandma to visit him daily. The first time we traveled down Main Street, it took me a second to identify the area where Jeff lived (or used to live, when I last saw him). Immediately, I was swept away by reminiscences, and I had to turn away to the window and close my eyes so my mom wouldn't see that I was trying not to cry. I feebly did the same thing the subsequent times I accompanied my mother to the hospital when we approached the neighbourhood, as if not seeing where he lived would keep me from getting emotional or remembering everything that had happened between us.

Or every time I saw the #33 bus: heading east, it was destined for 29th Avenue Station, where Sam lived, and conversely, to UBC, which he used to attend. Coal Harbour was the site of our first date. I squinted into the windshields of every compact, red four-door car, expecting to see Sam's face at the wheel.

There were also invisible, abstract mines: a mention of sea creatures, Joni Mitchell, Shakira, Vanessa Carlton songs I once serenaded Sam and G. with that I now refused to play. El Salvador. Spanish. I found G. on Grindr one day and though it had been years since we had broken up, I discovered that I still experienced slight anxiety—faster heart rate, shallow breaths—with the mere brief glimpse of his profile (which I had to block because I couldn't handle constantly and paranoically checking every square in sheer fear and dread).

Everywhere I went, there were the phantoms of happier times, of those who had moved on without me. I felt trapped, as if any and every step I took outside my front door had the possibility of mentally ending me for good. It was like a form of torture designed to break a prisoner's mind and spirit, except the guards had all retired and I had been abandoned there, screaming and crying at the images of memories that would never stop flashing before my pried-open eyes.

Slow as the shifting of the earth, things seemed to improve. I could go to school and work and at least function somewhat normally. Then, out of nowhere, thoughts would burst open like the evils from Pandora's box and circle me every waking moment. Lasting several days, rumination was so intense and so frequent that I found it impossible to concentrate on work or school; none of the things that were distractions, like work, helped. All day long, I imagined G. having sex with someone who wasn't me, kissing someone who wasn't me. In those instances, I had an inexplicable urge to hurl myself against a wall (which I never did, mostly for silly practical reasons like noise and possible damage). By the end of the night, I was mentally exhausted and defeated, yet I knew the cycle would only begin once more the following morning. I sat in one of my classes, on one occasion, binder out and ready to take notes, except my brain was being bombarded with images of the past. Before I knew it, an hour and a half had somehow gone by and I had absolutely no idea what had been taught. Times like these made me want to crawl into a corner and bawl. I half-joked to someone I was seeing that I wanted a lobotomy; I wanted so badly to simply cut the ache out of my head because it was unbearable.

While walking home after yet another one of these emotionally draining nights, I noticed the pale grey moon suspended against the darkened sky. *They say people and animals act differently around a full moon,* I recalled. Sure enough, the following instance I ruminated like a madman, I observed a full moon shining through a thin veil of clouds. I called this my PMS: for a few consecutive days every month without fail, I became someone, something, else that I couldn't seem to stop. The only thing I could do was hope—that I would survive yet another round of mental trauma.

There are mines that, like wounds, eventually heal. They may be deactivated, but walking around is precarious, tentative. One afternoon, I was hanging out with coworkers, strolling by Coal Harbour, when we happened by the same convenience store where Sam had bought an umbrella on our first date. It was impossible not to think of him as I walked past, but the sadness wasn't debilitating like it used to be. It was more of a nostalgic melancholy. It made me miss him.

These mines have detonated and might not cause any more ache, such as with my PMS which I thankfully no longer experience, but when I come across these places and objects, they are not so much mines but craters that remain from the explosion. When I recall the location's significance, it makes me shiver for some reason. I think I have become numb to the pain, like having a paralyzed limb. I carry around mental scars, and I am tired of remembering everything, of the constant prompts that assault me like a never-ending string of pop-up ads. I am tired of the mental equivalent of sobbing for days.

I am so run-down, my emotions so spent, I don't know if I can feel anything besides indifference for the city I once loved to explore.

I remember strawberry lollipops from the barber in Chinatown while waiting for my mom to pick me up after getting my hair cut. Mrs. Clarkson, my second-grade teacher, used to give me a few quarters to buy Mr. Freeze freezies—grape was my flavour of choice—from the school cafeteria. I deemed pretty much everyone in my elementary school classes a friend (which, in retrospect, was amazing considering I am an introvert now). One time, my sister was stung by a bee while we were walking down the street in Kerrisdale. My mom immediately rushed us into a nearby herbal remedy shop, and the staff applied ointment to Maggie's sting without expecting compensation. Everyone I knew and met seemed friendly, open, and approachable.

Get on board a bus or SkyTrain these days and the sight's guaranteed to be the same: people preferring to flip through their friends' Instagram stories or to play mobile games on their smartphones than, god forbid, make eye contact with other humans. I have a friend who brings a book to read on the bus for the sole purpose of avoiding people's gazes. One Grindr user and newcomer to the city lamented in his profile how everyone in Vancouver was cold. I couldn't help but agree with him.

What happened between then and now? It could entirely be that kids have rosy paintings of people when they are young, and/or how adults treat children nicer than one another. Or maybe adult life in Vancouver has always been this way.

I find it difficult to explain my dislike for Vancouverites. I think part of it has built up over many, many years: a lifetime's worth of nudges, pushes, shoves, and shoes on my feet without so much as a "sorry" or "excuse me," as if these phrases were not part of their vocabulary; all the times I have seen or dealt with ungrateful, rude, and disrespectful people in public—which is more than I can count—seem to outweigh all the neutral or positive experiences with strangers I have had. I have witnessed pedestrians refusing to get off buses and holding everyone up after wrongly boarding from the back doors; heard cars honk back at those who honk at them. And what is it with no one understanding how to correctly open the back doors of trolleybuses? (They're sensor-activated, not pressure-activated, so pushing on the door won't do anything except trigger a ringing alarm.) If you're lucky, you can catch a man who often stands on the corner of Broadway and

Commercial and yells epithets and hate speech for seemingly hours on end while everyone walks around him, wordless. On the night of my Creative Writing graduation party, a woman lambasted me in front of a bus-full of people, including my classmates, for not giving up my seat to an elderly couple I couldn't see (the couple was also behind a crowd of people several feet away and refused a seat in the end).

A co-worker of mine, who also isn't a fan of Vancouverites, told me, "It's hard to be nice when everyone around you isn't." And I want to be nice. I really do. It would be so much easier if I swore at drivers who don't check for pedestrians as they turned, for instance. I almost did, just today. I sense my niceness and patience dissolving, and it makes me disappointed because I never thought it could happen to me, but it has: the city has beaten me down.

This borderline hostile attitude has seeped its way across the town too. Most people don't seem to know that the gay community, despite how welcoming they are often portrayed as, can also be unfriendly. A teaching assistant for a Critical Studies in Sexuality class I took at UBC, who was also Asian and gay, related how he was outside of a club for a smoke one evening. When he realized he had left his lighter at home, he asked a white guy standing nearby if he had one. Immediately, the white dude took a step back and blurted, "I'm not into Asians!"

I had been more than familiar with racism in the gay community but up until then, I hadn't heard about people uttering racist statements outside gay dating apps or sites. To learn that racism had apparently manifested itself from subtle and suggested to explicit and everyday made me feel ashamed that it was happening in Vancouver, in a city where diversity is supposed to be celebrated as a Canadian value. After years of reading every issue, I had enough of the lack of people of colour in *Xtra!* and ultimately gave up on reading it altogether. I drifted further and further away from the community I once felt so close to (or believed I felt close to).

During my teenage years, I believed that when I got old enough to date, I would find other gay guys out there like me—romantic, intellectual, witty. Different. But more and more, it seemed like most gays in Vancouver were cut from the same cloth: interested in typical gay things such as working out, Top 40/dance music, muscles, selfies, thinking and talking about working out, aversion to reading and femininity, texting/typing/speaking in monosyllables ("Hi," "Hey," "Sup"), and of course, working out. I have lost count of how many conversations I have had that were in fact interviews— me asking them questions ("Where are you from?", "What do you do?", "What're some of your favourite movies?") until I grew bored. When guys mention, "Say hi!" or "Ask me anything!" on their profile, I suppose it means that they love to talk—about themselves.

I know someone who has what he calls a "Six Line Rule": "I give the conversation six lines and if it's boring or if it's one-way, then I stop," he explained. The rule, as harsh as it might seem, sounded reasonable to me, although the fact that such a rule even needed to exist was sad. Whether it be OKCupid or Grindr or Craigslist (I don't meet guys in person because I have no gaydar and guys don't talk to me), at a certain point, guys come off as simply uninteresting. I consider a lot of them to be basic gays. And again, it is disappointing more than anything. I genuinely feel like I won't meet my long-term romantic partner in Vancouver.

My friend John, originally from New Brunswick, says that he finds it difficult to date people here, especially those who are from Metro Vancouver: "I find that it's easier to talk to and connect to people who aren't from Vancouver. Vancouverites seem to be more closed for some reason."

I hadn't really observed this, but upon reflection, it does seem to me that a lot of people in Vancouver keep to themselves. If someone were to get chatted up by a stranger in public, say, on a bus, most people probably think something along the lines of, *Who are you and why are you talking to me and what the fuck do you really want please stop talking right now or else how do I get away from you?"*

Maybe this is a symptom of living in metropolises in North America—people in most major cities have this view as well. John believes that people are so wrapped up in their own hectic lives that city life becomes less community-oriented and more individualistic. Cities are always moving, and people are moving along with them. Talking to a stranger feels like halting the pulse and rhythm of a city.

Since Vancouverites seem so hesitant to connect to each other, it is no wonder I have also had such trouble dating. Messages are replied to without haste, dates never achieve confirmation and even when they do, I expect a high chance of flakiness. It seems like people see putting in time and effort to arrange a date as coming on too strong—too much, too fast, which is absurd and so frustrating, unless they plan on limiting any and all interactions with humans via WhatsApp.

The last guy I was interested in was Daniel (the same one from "In the Dust" who, after we had one date, got back together with his ex-boyfriend). Two years later, I stumbled upon his familiar face in a square on Grindr. His status was listed as single. I said hi, expecting him to ignore me, and was surprised and glad when he responded.

We made dinner plans for dosas at an Indian restaurant in East Van. On the day of our date, I found myself getting nervous. Was it going to be awkward, especially because of the way he abruptly ended things those years ago? What if we didn't get along like before?

Those doubts dissipated when I stepped into the restaurant and we hugged. He looked the same—still handsome with his short dark hair, facial hair, and eyes that looked equally good with or without his glasses. Conversation came naturally, as it did the first time around; it took us a while to stop talking long enough to flag down a server and order food. I felt silly to have been so anxious.

"So why did you ask me out again?" Daniel asked.

I thought for a moment. "I thought we got along really well and we had a good time. And... I like you."

He smiled at me. "Well, I'm glad you contacted me. Do you remember our first date?"

I froze. I assumed he was not going to talk about it. At least I wasn't.

I said I did. "Do you?"

"Don't tell me. We watched a movie... *Spirited Away*. And

then we went for cheesecake at... Trees, no, it was Cafe Artigiano."

"Close. It was actually *Kiki's Delivery Service*. And it was Trees, not Artigiano."

"Right, right. I thought it was Trees. But I remember we had cheesecake on the patio, on the right side of the cafe, second table in."

We bonded over our shared curiosity of the difference between "assume" and "presume" (which led to Daniel looking up the definitions on his phone); our homesteading activities (he made salves and wanted to try his hand at producing essential oils while I told him about the various kinds of bar soaps I used to make); both of us being cat owners whose pets sleep with us at night, and the weird but hilarious thing he did of licking/grooming his cat back; and our mutual interest in writing as a career. Our dinner felt like a classic example of a great first-date montage: there were jokes, wit, humour, chemistry. Daniel was one of the few people who easily brought out that outgoing side of me, the side that few people ever saw (on dates or otherwise).

When we finished our meals, Daniel looked at me. "You're quieter than you were last time," he commented.

Maybe because I'm watching what I'm saying. I simply stared at him. *You. Are. Wonderful. Just. Wonderful.*

"Are you trying to put together what you're thinking into words?"

"No. Are you?"

"Yes." He paused and pursed his lips. "Would you like to go out on a second date?"

I continued to stare at him without a change of expression, attempting to create suspense. Finally, I answered with a nonchalant, "Okay."

We both grinned. *He likes me! He likes me!* the little romantic boy inside me cried with glee.

After I paid for dinner (for both of us), we went outside to the chill of West Coast winter. Daniel's jacket looked like it was more suited for spring; to my disappointment, my fleece lined jacket didn't insulate me well enough either.

"Are you going up to take the bus home? I can escort you, and then I'm just going to walk home," Daniel said.

Feeling assertive, I replied, "I can walk you home if you want."

"You sure? That would be great."

As we strolled through East Van, our hands brushed against one another's. I fought the urge to take and hold it, certain it would (fatally) come across as moving too quickly. When we arrived at Daniel's place, the basement suite of a house, he inquired, "Do you want to come in and warm up a bit? I'm going to use the bathroom and then I'll say goodnight to you." I said sure.

I waited in his room and gazed at everything—his collection of Isaac Asimov paperbacks stacked in a corner, guitar sheet music, and piles of clothes on the floor.

"I see you're a fan of Asimov. I've never read any," I said when Daniel returned.

"Oh, yeah. He's great. Do you want to borrow one?" he asked, smiling.

"Um... maybe next time."

"Sure. Ready to go?"

Daniel accompanied me back to the door. "I had a good time," he said.

"I did too."

"Come here." With that, Daniel opened his arms. We hugged for a few moments, and when we broke, we remained close.

He laughed. "I actually didn't mean a hug. I meant this."

In what seemed like slow motion to me, his eyes closed and his face leaned in to mine. I closed my eyes as well and felt his lips. We kissed for a second—when suddenly he pulled away.

"This is okay, right? I just have to ask."

I chuckled. "Yeah, it's fine." We went back to kissing. In what was likely only ten seconds or so, I developed an insta-boner that I then hastily and clumsily tried to conceal/smother as we made plans for later that week and wished each other goodnight. Instead of catching the bus, I walked home, giddy and grinning like a schoolboy who had had his first kiss.

"Looking forward to this Friday :)," Daniel texted.

Throughout the next few days, I intentionally limited my messages with Daniel, aware that in the past, others I had dated had found it suffocating. By the end of the week, I was acing this round of a game I had constantly lost. I was determined to win this time.

We had made plans to watch *The Forbidden Room* (my suggestion) at the site of our first date, The Cinematheque, but hadn't decided what time to meet, so on the day of what was supposed to be my first second date in god knows how long, I texted Daniel.

"Are we still on for a movie tonight?"

"Did you not get my text?"

"No. Can you not come tonight?"

"Worse."

Daniel re-sent his text from earlier: in it, he mentioned that he didn't want to date me. He apologized profusely for leading me on and toying with my emotions, and that the kiss was unplanned and "not an accurate reflection of what I want."

I wasn't sure what to think or feel, besides crushing disappointment. The only thing I could come up with was, *But why?* So I asked why.

"I've just been doing a lot of thinking about where I am in life, and it's not what I want." Although I am gullible quite often, I couldn't help but think that was the most bullshit reason someone could give.

When I asked if he would like to keep in touch or to never see me again, he replied, "If I had to choose, I'd say never see you again."

"I don't know if I can trust anything you say anymore," I responded, then realized how weak and pathetic my words were since he would never say anything else to me anyway.

And that was that. For the next few days, I furiously ruminated and pondered why Daniel broke it off forever: Did he find my blog with me posing in my underwear with books I had read? Did he read that bathhouse story I wrote and thought I was a giant slut? Or was it that sexual comment I made the night before our second date when I texted him saying I expected the Vanessa Carlton concert to give me an orgasm (because I was a mega fan and had never seen her perform live)? Was he bothered by the fact that I work on-call at the library and thus, don't have a regular work schedule? Or that I still lived at home? Did he have a problem with the fact that I was hesitant about going on a Working Holiday—or perhaps he found my pessimism unattractive when I confided that I didn't write poetry anymore because my poems don't get published? Did someone else come along? Not knowing the true reason bothered the hell out of me. It also made me incredibly sad that he said he never wanted to see me again, as if I had done something irredeemable, unforgiveable, or that there was something fundamentally wrong with me that even friendship was not worth salvaging. There are times when I think of him and what happened and it still makes me tear up because I genuinely liked him a lot.

To me, Daniel exemplified the typical Vancouverite: he was friendly and clever after getting to know him, but he could also be cold and impenetrable. He represented another broken connection in Vancouver among the assholes, racists, and unfriendly people.

When I come across someone who tells me they are new to Vancouver, be it a Grindr profile or a new co-worker, my first thought is, *Why?*

My second thought is *Get out. Get out while you still can.*

While heading home via the SkyTrain one afternoon, I overheard two guys talking. I wasn't paying attention to what they were saying until one of them asked the other, "How many of your friends are from Vancouver? Like, actually born here?"

"Um, I know a surprising amount of Calgarians," which didn't answer the question at all and yet, at the same time, answered it perfectly.

Vancouver natives are few and far between in the city. Whenever I meet someone who is born and raised here like me, there is a sense of camaraderie, like discovering a long lost relative (Conversations usually go something like this: "You're from Vancouver? Born and raised?" "Yeah! You too?" "Yeah!").

It makes me wonder where they have all gone. All my former schoolmates—what happened to them? Are they out in smaller, closer-knit towns where everybody knows each other's names and leaves their doors unlocked? Or have they relocated to warmer climates with kilometres of scorching sand and sunshine? Or have they simply moved to another mega-city, crowded with bodies yet void of authentic human contact?

Most importantly, are they happy they left?

The permanent aroma of coffee beans and hissing espresso machines flooded my senses as I heaved my cumbersome keyboard into Trees Organic Coffee. I was scheduled to perform alongside two other singer-songwriters, both of whom were guitarists, at one of their weekly live music nights. This was nothing new; I appeared destined to be the piano guy wherever I went, which I was more than happy to be.

When the first musician finished his set, I noticed a few of the audience members going up to and conversing with him. Interactions like that rarely happened to me, and I held back a quiet pang of jealousy.

My small group of friends crammed themselves together at a couple tables near the front and cheered me on as I took the stage and introduced myself. I left my friend Bekki in charge of selling copies of my demo if anyone wanted to buy them (instead of a set price, they were available by donation). Six songs and a parched mouth later, I returned to my friends.

No one from the audience came and talked to me the rest of the night. No one bought any copies of my demo.

I thought that night might have been a one-off, but I noticed the identical scenario playing out again and again. I would get up onstage, do my little act, get off, and usually go home without incident. That was what bothered me: nothing was happening. Nobody seemed to take notice.

Sure, I was able to give away copies of my demo and perform for people, which was always a blast, but there didn't seem to be any progress. I was not making connections; no one chatted with me about music or what I was doing or invited me to do some gigs or offered me a record deal (ha). And being young, I was nervous. I had no clue who to talk to, so I waited for people to approach me. Which they rarely did.

Maybe I took what I was doing too seriously while others didn't take me seriously enough. Eventually, I felt the truth in my gut one day: I will never be as famous or successful as I wanted to be as a musician.

So, after a few years of performing and writing music, I stopped. Vancouver didn't seem to care. I was only one out of how many dozens of musicians here? *This is a city of broken dreams, baby,* I could hear Vancouver whispering in my ear as she returned to nurturing other hopeless ambitions.

When film entered my life, I was re-inspired. This was an opportunity to start with a blank slate, to amend the mistakes I had made as a musician, like trying harder to network and getting my name out there more by spamming my friends and the measly handful of people in my social networks.

Things began well enough. *On the Bus* screened at a whole bunch of film festivals around the world, much to my amazement. I attended the Vancouver Queer Film Festival's after-party with other local directors and forced myself to approach people and strike up conversations. I was proud of myself for doing something that terrified me (especially as an introvert). However, when the organizers at film festivals contacted me to let me know *On the Bus* had been accepted, they often said, "Congrats! We would like to talk to the director now."

With that, I became a director and somehow managed to make *Stay*. It was accepted into fewer film festivals than *On the Bus*, but since I was the director, I was interviewed by local media and publications, met new people at the afterparty (and was also introduced to some by colleagues). All this made me genuinely believe I could make it as a filmmaker.

Unfortunately, the feeling was short-lived. Each subsequent film I made created less of a splash than the previous; there were fewer acceptances into film festivals, fewer people who wanted to talk to me, less press. I tried to stay positive and to persevere, but I could hear that doubtful, niggling voice murmuring in the background once more (as well as literally in the foreground; my parents relentlessly urged me to do something, anything else that was more lucrative). I didn't want to feel like I had failed another creative career.

Every year at the Closing Gala of the Vancouver Queer Film Festival, I held my breath in anticipation as they announced the winners of the short film awards. And every year, they called someone else's names and films. I didn't make films to win awards, but at the Closing Gala, I always believed there was a possibility that I could win something; I would be lying if I said those awards didn't mean anything to me. There was a monetary prize, sure, but more importantly, they meant recognition. I had been making films without much feedback from audiences, so an award indicated people enjoyed my film and/or recognized its artistic merit. Validation.

As I continued making movies that fewer and fewer people watched, the nagging feeling that I was traveling down the same route as my music "career" continued to elbow me in the side. Furthermore, filmmaking cost money and lots of time and planning; I was still a full-time college student at the time—and not even studying film—so it was always a substantial side project and undertaking in my life.

Upon making *Anniversary*, I met with two producers and my cinematographer to talk about options for my next film. It was a toss-up between two scripts I had written: one was a time travel story about regret and the other, a silent film featuring a ghost and his lover. Personally, I was more attached to the ghost story but having said that, the time travel script was more of a conventional narrative film, less experimental. I could see it going over well at film festivals and with general audiences.

One of the producers asked me which script I wanted to

shoot, and I explained my predicament. "Well, you have to decide: do you want to make a film that wins awards or do you want to make a film that you want to make? It ultimately depends on what your goals are."

I considered this. My goal had always been to make good films and to tell stories to which I had an emotional connection. But if other people didn't feel strongly about my work or didn't connect with it or worse, didn't watch it, would I not be making a film for myself? What was the point in that, after all the effort in organizing and filming?

"Let's go with the time travel one," I announced.

We began discussing plans. As the three of them talked about assembling crew members and possible locations, I continued mulling over what she had told me. Had I become one of those artists that valued popularity over artistic integrity?

I interrupted everyone. "Actually, I changed my mind. I want to do the ghost one."

The producer gave me a smile, like I had picked the correct one.

While prepping for and shooting *June*, I made the decision that any future projects hinged on the success of this film. If it did well, I might continue making further films. If it did not, I would likely take a break for an indeterminate length of time while I focused on my studies.

June became the short film that I spent the most time, money, and effort making. I rented equipment from a professional production company, something I had never done for my previous projects. With the help of friends, I launched a crowdfunding campaign. We spent months scouring possible locations before finding and paying the owner of a home in Coquitlam to allow us to film there for two days. Chelsea and I went shopping and bought groceries to make meals for the cast and crew. Extensive auditions were held to find the right actors; it took an absurd amount of time scheduling days that worked for everyone.

Fast forward some months. The film was shot, edited, scored. I hired a sound editor to ensure the audio and sound design were absolutely perfect. While editing, there were times when I teared up watching it (which I took as a good emotional sign rather than being in love with my own art). I considered *June* the best, most personal film I made.

As with my other films, *June* was set to make its world premiere at the Vancouver Queer Film Festival in August at the Rio Theatre in front of a full house. The screening itself was uneventful, if anything; the cast and crew hung out after and celebrated over beers.

A week or so later, the Closing Gala rolled around. That evening, I sat trembling with apprehension in a plush but cramped seat at the Vancouver Playhouse. When the jury got up on stage to announce the winners of the awards, I held my breath again. *Remember: no expectations,* I told myself. I wasn't sure if I believed it or not.

"All of us jury members had different films at the top of our lists," they said. "But there was one that showed up on each of ours."

Then I heard them say unfamiliar words—words of another film. I clapped politely alongside everyone, half-relieved that the moment was over as I exhaled. Nonetheless, the news confirmed that my affair with filmmaking was a casual fling than a long-term commitment.

June screened at a fraction of the festivals *On the Bus* screened at. This project that had been a part of me for years—from idea, to planning, to filming, to editing, to debut—didn't seem to resonate all that much with the rest of the world. Then again, did I really expect people to enjoy a six-minute silent movie? Letting go was disheartening, but the sadness was not grief so much as it was like waving goodbye to a friend you likely wouldn't see again.

Presently, I have a rewarding enough day-job as a library assistant and media lab technician at the Vancouver Public Library, which also gives me time to write, fortunately, but if this writing thing doesn't work out, I am not sure what to do. Maybe this book will perform like my music demos and no one will purchase it. Or perhaps, like my short films, it will be noticed by some, only to fade away into obscurity and become another dusty, forgotten book on a shelf at the library.

I am aware enough to recognize that writing is a much more feasible hobby than filmmaking (writing is free!) but still, it is a considerable undertaking. James Patterson I am not, brimming with a billion plans for stories, or have an insatiable drive to constantly be writing or else I am unable to function. If I could no longer write, I could live. There have been times when I have taken hiatuses from writing this book and it has been completely fine and relaxing to not have to sit on my ass for hours staring at my laptop. Writing is not life or death.

Sometimes, I wonder if it might be easier and better to give up all this artsy stuff and get a stable, full-time office job somewhere, one that isn't dependent on luck and connections. I imagine myself in a confined, heaven-white cubicle with a shirt and tie, typing away on my desktop computer. Someone trots by—I want to call him Ted for some reason—and asks for a report. I tell Ted I am working on it, but that it is a little dry and boring.

"You're a writer. Be creative!" he says, accompanied by bro slaps on the back.

"I don't do that anymore," I'll mutter.

Back in 2009, I was invited to participate in a panel at the Sprockets Film Festival in Toronto for *On the Bus*. I had briefly visited the city years ago on a short East Coast tour; my family and I were there for less than a day. Aside from some vicarious animosity for Toronto thanks to my fellow Vancouverites ("Toronto thinks it's the centre of the universe," my sister used to sneer), I didn't have strong feelings one way or another about the city. I thought Toronto was going to be a bigger Vancouver.

As I ambled through downtown amongst cathedrals of towers, buildings, and stores, pushed through metal turnstiles to get to the shrieking subway trains, and meandered past houses and schools, I experienced something curious.

I could genuinely see myself living there.

This sensation never arose when I had visited London or New York or Honolulu or anywhere else. Toronto felt like home. There was no other way to describe it.

Three years later, I traveled with my mom and sister to Asia for the first time, with our final week in Hong Kong. Perhaps it was how unchallenging it was navigating dense Hong Kong, or that I could detect the heartbeat of the perpetually moving city, or that I was surrounded by people who looked like me, whom I could semi-communicate with, or how modern everything was—the identical feeling I experienced in Toronto stirred within me again.

I could live here.

Something about those two cities made me believe I could be content living there. Of course, it could have merely been a silly, ephemeral feeling that meant absolutely nothing (maybe it was my stomach demanding me to feed it?). I certainly hadn't experienced it in Vancouver, at least in recent years. Maybe I used to when I was younger and simply grew accustomed to it. Or perhaps I never had it at all.

It was also overseas that I had the opportunity and freedom to walk around a city without anxiety. Everything was untarnished and unexplored, so there were no mines. G. rarely, if ever, crossed my mind; there was only a brief moment in the airport when I glimpsed the back of someone's head that bore a resemblance to his that a sickening jolt temporarily stunned me.

Life could be lived without debilitating mental anguish after all. I dreaded returning to Vancouver, where the minefield awaited me once more. I knew I deserved better.

In all my years here, I don't know how many people I have met in Vancouver who have told me, "I used to live in [insert city]. Then I came to Vancouver and I love it."

Their starry-eyed enthusiasm for such a dreadful, boring place has always befuddled me. It made me wonder why they had left their hometowns; if Vancouver was such a utopia, what did that say about where they came from?

That being said, if I were a newcomer to Vancouver, I could see how the mountain and ocean scenery, mild seasonal weather, fresh air, great cuisine, and diversity could impress and entrance someone enough to make them stay permanently. I wish I possessed such profound wonder for my own city.

One night, on an impulse to utilize the sauna at a gay bathhouse—*It'll be good for my eczema*, I told myself—I was engaging with the genial older gentleman behind the counter. I had spoken with him on a few previous occasions, but knew nothing about him.

"I hear an accent in your voice. Where are you from?" I asked.

"Europe."

"Where in Europe?"

"Hungary."

In true Vancouverite fashion, he mentioned how he had been living in Vancouver for years and raved about what a wonderful city it was. When I told him that I didn't find it so great and that I was writing a memoir detailing exactly how not great it was, he had this to say.

"After you live somewhere else for a while, you will see that Vancouver is better in a lot of ways."

I think he had a point. I haven't lived anywhere else in my thirty years on this planet. Maybe then, I can restart—and appreciate the scenery, the people, all over again. I might be able to date someone elsewhere. Maybe then, this minefield of a city will be purged of its concealed bombs and haunting memories and I will be able to live in—and love—my hometown like I once did all those years ago. Like so many people currently do.

Vancouver will not move.

So I have to.

Publication credits

The following pieces have appeared in various publications, many in different or slightly different forms: "In the Movies" was published in *Wilde,* Issue 4; "Between Channels" was published in *Existere,* Volume 33, Issue 2; "The World Behind Closed Doors" was published in *Ricepaper,* Issue 19.1 (printed as "Behind Closed Doors"); "A Case of Jeff" won *subTerrain*'s Lush Triumphant Literary Award in Creative NonFiction in 2013 and was published in Issue 66; "Cold War" was published in *Ricepaper,* Issue 20.1; "Underworld" was published in *Plenitude*; "The Birth and Death of You and Me" was published in *filling station,* Issue 62; "Identities" was published on dailyxtra.com.

Acknowledgements

This book was written on the unceded Coast Salish territories of the Musqueam, Squamish, and Tsleil-Waututh people.

Without the guidance of Andreas Schroeder and his creative non-fiction class at the University of British Columbia, this book would not exist. I had no plans to write a memoir collection until I took your class. Thank you so much for your invaluable mentorship, feedback, and for inspiring me to write this book.

To Marshall Moore, who took my manuscript and believed in it when I was beginning not to. Thank you for your work and your patience with me, and thank you to the other folks at Signal 8.

To my friends and fellow writers who helped read parts of this book as it developed: Haley, Wendy, Stefan, Deborah, Devon. To my colleagues for keeping me going: Amber Dawn, Candie, John R., Dana, Diana, Roberto, Karl, Kerri, Arhea.

To my friends Chelsea, Annie, Ayden, Dan YC, Dave: thank you for all your unconditional love and support, especially when I considered abandoning this project many, many times. You are my family. To my Dan, I don't know how I found you, but I'm so grateful to have you in my life. And to Curtis, the man in the background of many of the events in this book. I will write our story someday. I love you and I miss you.

To my cat Batman for always being there for me and quietly keeping me company while I wrote this book and sent it out. You're a great companion.

To Mom and Dad for your patronage. I hope I can make

you proud one day. I suppose I should thank my sisters here too.

To Manuela and Cristian for the lovely cover art.

And to you, dear reader. I may have things published, but I have never felt like people want to read my work. If you have made it this far (do people even read the Acknowledgements page?) and something in these pages has resonated with you, that's more than I could ever hope for. Thank you for giving me and this book your time.

Lightning Source UK Ltd.
Milton Keynes UK
UKHW021401130921
390500UK00015B/1254

9 789887 794912